Mentoring: Creating Connected, Empowered Relationships

By Valerie L. Schwiebert

With contributions from
Catherine Y. Chang, Mary D. Deck,
Penny Smith, June Williams, and Cathy Woodyard

MENTORING: CREATING CONNECTED, EMPOWERED RELATIONSHIPS

10 9 8 7 6 5 4 3 2 1

American Counseling Association
5999 Stevenson Avenue
Alexandria, VA 22304

Director of Publications
Carolyn C. Baker

Copy editor
Sharon Doyle

Cover design by Spot Color

Library of Congress Cataloging-in-Publication Data

Schwiebert, Valerie L.
    Mentoring : creating connected, empowered relationships / by Valerie L. Schwiebert.
      p. cm.
    Includes bibliographical references and index.
    ISBN 1-55620-223-7 (alk. paper)
      1. Counseling. 2. Mentoring. I. Title
  BF637.C6 S37 2000
  158'.3—dc21   99-045898

Table of Contents

Acknowledgments

I thank my wonderful family, Ryan, Kristi, Alexis, and Bryanna, for their unconditional love, support, and encouragement. I also thank my friend and colleague, Judy Revere, for her editorial assistance, friendship, and cheerleading and my terrific editor, Carolyn Baker, for supporting this project and making the difficult task of writing a book much easier. Finally, I thank my mentors for their continuing influence in my life and the lives of others. Without all of these individuals, this book would never have been completed.

Dedication

To Jane E. Myers, my mentor for life,
with love, admiration, and gratitude.

Foreword

By Jane E. Myers

*I*t was with great pleasure that I accepted Valerie Schwiebert's offer to write the foreword for this book. I was intrigued by the title, eager to read the best thinking of Dr. Schwiebert and her capable contributors on a little-understood topic, and curious about what I might learn as I read the manuscript in preparation for my contribution. Overall, it has been a rewarding experience, evoking thoughts, feelings, memories, hopes, and desires concerning my own past, present, and anticipated future mentoring experiences. These experiences have, at a minimum, the dual focus of roles as mentor and mentee while also stimulating the counselor educator side of me to ask the following question: How can we train counselors to be effective mentors to others?

As I read the manuscript, I was impressed with the broad scope of literature reviewed and assimilated in each chapter. A historical overview of mentoring sets the stage for examining the evolution of mentoring as a phenomenon of modern times. A review of cross-disciplinary research and theory, woven throughout the chapters of the book, provides a basis for applying mentoring concepts within the helping professions. Thus, a scientific lens is provided for the reader to explore the purpose, process, and outcomes of the phenomenon known as mentoring. This lens incorporates a multicultural perspective, with concepts of gender issues in mentoring both underscored and explored.

In addition to providing a scientific perspective, the authors present their personal stories of mentoring relationships. In these narratives, the reader finds compelling evidence of the power and singular importance of the topic. Mentors are shown to be critical factors underlying successful career paths. In addition, mentors are depicted as human and imperfect yet also as examples of integrity that inspire personal growth through challenge, encouragement, and modeling of behaviors.

I was especially pleased to note the emphasis on mentoring as a process—not as an event or an outcome—in which those involved, mentor as well as mentee, can and do change over time. The cornerstone of mentoring lies in the relationship between mentor and mentee. As is true of virtually all relationships, this special folie à deux of necessity develops and changes over time. Both mentor and mentee are affected as they mutually direct and experience these changes in a reciprocal relationship in which both derive ultimate benefit.

As I read through the chapters of the book, arranged in a helpful sequence that continually provoked and expanded my thinking about the topic, several lines of questioning emerged. First, I found myself thinking about my own experiences with mentors. These experiences were primarily haphazard and unplanned, yet fortunate overall. Trying to think retrospectively, I attempted to answer questions such as "How did these mentors become part of my life?" "What were the critical incidents and experiences?" and "How might my career and personal life have been different had mentors not been present at significant, teachable moments?" As I thought about the impact of the various mentors in my life, considered the stories of the authors, and reviewed the research presented, several additional questions emerged. The answers to these questions are woven in a tapestry throughout the book and point to needed areas of research relevant to mentoring, such as

How does a willing mentee find a suitable mentor?
How does a willing mentor find a mentee?
Can mentors be assigned?
What are the dynamics of an *intentional* mentoring process?
How are these dynamics similar to or different from those mentoring relationships that develop naturally or accidentally?
What are the characteristics of good mentors? How can a person develop those characteristics? Can they be taught?

What is the importance of mentoring in various roles and settings?

What kinds of qualitative and quantitative research studies are needed to more fully explore the dynamics of mentoring and provide needed guidelines for this process?

Overall, I was struck in my reading with the fact that this book is long overdue. It speaks to a powerful process that is life-changing. Such a process cannot be left to chance but should be encouraged and fostered through intentional developmental processes that establish the types of connected relationships that Schwiebert and others write about so powerfully in this text. The creative process—establishing mentoring relationships where none have existed before—requires concerted effort grounded in a base of knowledge and experience. That base is clearly, consistently, and sensitively provided in this book. The reader who is fortunate to encounter this book is invited into a world that promises to help him or her "create connected, empowered relationships" that will lead to positive life change, personally and professionally. Enjoy the journey!

Jane E. Myers, PhD, LPC
Professor, Counselor Education
University of North Carolina at Greensboro

Introduction

By Valerie L. Schwiebert

Mentoring: Creating Connected, Empowered Relationships is the culmination of collaborative efforts across disciplines, genders, and generations. The seeds for the topics contained in this book were first planted as I began my life's journey. I have been fortunate to encounter many mentors throughout my journey, some of whom have joined me for short periods whereas others continue to walk with me, all of them affecting the sum total of who and where I am. My mentors from an early age included my father, my aunt, and grade school teachers who believed in me.

My father taught me powerful lessons, which have served me throughout my life. Surviving my mother's death and having been left with two young children, my younger brother and me, my father did not give up. He worked hard to create a family and to be both mother and father. Through his example, I learned both strength and nurturance, and I learned that both qualities can exist in one gender. He taught me that it was who I was, not my gender, that determined what I could do and whom I would become. He always encouraged me to try, teaching me to believe in myself and instilling the idea that I could do anything if I would only try. These lessons have served me well throughout my life and continue to be a source of strength. I often have thought, as I work with my clients, how different their lives might have been had someone instilled the same ideas in them.

My aunt served as my surrogate mother and mentor. She taught me to laugh and to enjoy life. She taught me to take chances. As a nursing professor, she modeled for me the balance between being a professional and a human being. She loved, cared for, and nurtured others regardless of their race, gender, or affliction. She was also professional, strong, and competent.

Several teachers and my high school guidance counselor also served as mentors and role models. They encouraged me to persevere even when I was experiencing great sadness and pain in my personal life. Both my brother and my aunt had been diagnosed with cancer, and my father had remarried a woman who was diagnosed with bipolar disorder and borderline personality disorder. Recognizing my struggle, my guidance counselor encouraged me to graduate from high school at age 16 and helped me enroll at the University of Florida. Without his recognition of my academic ability, my personal turmoil, and the negative direction my life could have taken had I not left that environment, I probably would not have finished high school and perhaps would not be here to write this book. Mr. Mello was an outstanding counselor and took great personal risks at that time to encourage me to do something that not only was nontraditional but also was not particularly thought of as an option for a young woman. He spent many hours with me discussing the benefits and limitations of different decisions and empowered me to make the right choice for myself. Thus began my journey in higher education.

It was not until I entered my doctoral program that I met my first professional and academic mentor, Dr. Jane E. Myers. As I struggled to find my way, she helped me to make sense out of my confusion. She provided guidance, strength, hope, and encouragement. She served as a role model for what a competent and professional woman could become. She used her power and position to help me negotiate the system, learn about my profession, and try on various professional roles. She challenged me to give my best and never settled for less. Even when she relocated to another university in another state, she continued to serve as my dissertation and doctoral program chairperson. Never more than a telephone call away, she continued to motivate me to become all that I could become, teaching me that I did not have to settle for an either/or identity—wife and mother or professional—but rather to strive for the fullness of life to which I aspired—wife, mother, and professional. Her mentoring did not end when I finished my doctoral degree.

By using her professional connections and reputation, she helped me gain entry into professional associations, provided me with references, and assisted me in finding a faculty position. Had it not been for her continued mentoring, I never would have survived my first few years as a beginning faculty member at a research one institution. I found myself in a very competitive, nonsupportive environment, surrounded by colleagues who believed in the "sink or swim" theory of initiating new faculty in a male-dominated system. Again, my mentor came to my rescue. She invited me to be a copresenter and coauthor. She provided consultation and shared her syllabi and course materials with me. As I began to grow and become more established in my position as a faculty member, she allowed our relationship to mature, and our relationship began to take on new components, that of colleague and friend. Though she will always be my mentor, we have seen the relationship come full circle. Once, when I asked her how I would ever be able to repay her for all she had done for me and all that she continues to do, she said, "Do more than I have done, achieve more than I have achieved." I believe therein lies the key to effective mentoring: to allow our protégés to find their own potentials; to be different from ourselves; to exceed our achievements; to celebrate their unique contributions; to resist the temptation to keep them as our subordinates and to limit them to our own achievements; and, finally, to allow the relationship to come full circle.

As this book began to take shape, I was given the opportunity to take on a new position at the University. I moved from my position on the counselor education faculty to an administrative position as Associate Dean of the Graduate School. Although I continue to serve on the counseling faculty, the shift from faculty member to administrator has been a challenging one. Again, I have been fortunate to have mentors who have encouraged me to make the shift and who continue to support me as I attempt to master my new roles and responsibilities. These mentors have provided me with new experiences in mentoring relationships as well. Two of my new mentors are White men in senior administrative positions (one in my field and one outside my field). One of my new mentors is a Black man in a senior administrative position. These new mentoring relationships have allowed me to experience firsthand the value of multiple mentoring models, cross-gender mentoring, and cross-cultural mentoring. These experiences also have reinforced for me the incredible power and importance of mentoring as a process for personal and professional growth.

It is from this beginning that the importance of mentoring has become apparent to me. I have been privileged to experience effective mentoring at many different levels from many different individuals, many of whom I have not named here. In an attempt to help others benefit from this powerful process, I have begun researching, presenting, and writing on the topic of mentoring. From presentations and articles focusing on women as mentors with my colleague, Mary Deck, I have been struck by the lack of available mentors and the great need that many persons, both male and female, have expressed for mentors. Even individuals who are perceived as very successful in their chosen careers report that, although they did not have a mentor, they would have liked to have had one, given the opportunity.

Therefore, I was incredibly excited to learn that Cathy Woodyard, editor for the Chi Sigma Iota International newsletter, *The Exemplar,* would be doing a special issue on the topic of mentoring. I offered to help, and as a result, she invited me to attend a meeting at the American Counseling Association Convention in Indianapolis, Indiana, to discuss mentoring and the special issue. As I sat around a table with women from diverse experiences and ages, it became apparent to me that there was a great deal of positive energy generated from a discussion of the topic of mentoring. The ideas that resulted were far too numerous and important to be included in one brief newsletter. Therefore, I agreed to serve as the catalyst for generating this book, a compilation of information on the topic of mentoring. The title was generated at the meeting as we discussed the ultimate purpose of the mentoring relationship. Although not all of the participants at the meeting chose to contribute chapters to this book, we would like to recognize their contribution to its spirit. Other contributing authors were not at the initial meeting but joined our efforts along the way. Their insights and interests have expanded the topic in still more directions. We hope that this book serves as a beginning toward more recognition of the importance of the mentoring process, particularly in the field of counseling. Even more important, we hope that this book will inspire you, the reader, to both provide and participate in mentoring relationships, which create connected, empowered relationships across genders, disciplines, and generations.

This book is organized in such a way as to present an overview of the history of mentoring in chapter 1, followed by a discussion of the traditional male model of mentoring in chapter 2. The overview provides the reader with a context for the following chapters by focusing on the past, present, and future of mentoring. The chapter on men and mentoring follows because the male model of mentoring has been the traditional approach to mentoring and because, historically, men have been the greatest beneficiaries of this process. Chapter 3 focuses on issues in cross-gender mentoring because they tend to represent the second most frequently occurring mentoring relationships. This chapter is followed by a discussion of women and mentoring in chapter 4. Barriers to mentoring relationships for and by women are discussed as well as strategies for women to begin to benefit from the use of mentoring, something that men have done for many years. This chapter is followed by chapter 5, a chapter on multicultural perspectives related to mentoring. Just as the traditional male model of mentoring may not fit well for women, it may not fit well for members of underrepresented groups. This chapter discusses the implications of mentoring for members of underrepresented groups. Programs and models of mentoring are presented in chapter 6, in which the focus is on presenting the reader with differing formal models of mentoring, emphasizing their strengths and weaknesses. Strategies for mentoring are outlined in chapter 7, which focuses on specific strategies for mentors and protégés to use in developing effective informal mentoring relationships. Professional development and mentoring in the field of counseling is the topic of chapter 8. This chapter discusses issues of mentoring directly related to the field of counseling and counselor education. Mentoring in educational settings is addressed in chapter 9. This chapter focuses on school counseling and mentoring. The book concludes with chapter 10, which provides a discussion of issues in mentoring. In this final chapter, important issues are revisited, and the discussion is brought to a close.

In each of the chapters, we have attempted to review the related professional literature augmented with personal examples and applications. It is important to note that even though the contributors to this book and I are female, and the literature suggests that women underutilize this valuable process, this book is intended to explore the mentoring process both for and by men and women. Additionally, the reader should note that this book is a beginning. It is our hope that it will serve as a catalyst to encourage the reader to look for examples of mentoring in his or her own life; to recognize the importance of mentoring relationships; and to initiate mentoring relationships in which he or she serves as mentor, protégé, or both. Now, as you begin reading, we invite you to enter into a dialogue with us related to the benefits, limitations, and implications of mentoring.

About the Authors

Valerie L. Schwiebert, PhD, is an Associate Professor of Counseling and Associate Dean of Research and Graduate Studies at Western Carolina University. Dr. Schwiebert received her master's degree in rehabilitation counseling, her specialist degree in counseling, and her doctorate in counselor education with a graduate certificate in gerontology from the University of Florida. Dr. Schwiebert has worked as a rehabilitation counselor, a mental health counselor in private practice, a researcher for the Area Agency on Aging, and an administrator of a substance abuse evaluation program for the state of Florida.

Dr. Schwiebert is a national certified counselor, a national certified gerontological counselor, a licensed professional counselor in North Carolina, and a certified rehabilitation counselor. She was president of the Illinois Association for Assessment in Counseling. Nationally, she is active in the Association for Adult Development and Aging (AADA), the Association for Assessment in Counseling, Chi Sigma Iota, and the Society of Research Administrators. She is the recipient of AADA and Chi Sigma Iota research awards for her research in the area of adult children providing caregiving for aging parents.

Dr. Schwiebert has written numerous articles and two books in the area of counseling older persons and adult children caring for aging parents.

Catherine Y. Chang, PhD, is an Assistant Professor of Counseling at Clemson University.

Mary D. Deck, PhD, is a Professor of Counseling at Western Carolina University.

Penny Smith, PhD, is an Associate Professor and Chairperson of Educational Leadership and Foundations at Western Carolina University.

June Williams, PhD, is the Assistant Dean of Student Life at South Eastern Louisiana University.

Cathy Woodyard, EdD, is an Assistant Professor of Counseling at Texas Woman's University.

CHAPTER

Mentoring: Past, Present, and Future

By Valerie L. Schwiebert

T he concept of mentoring is an old one, dating back to Greek mythology and first appearing in the book *The Odyssey* by Homer (1919). In this work, Athena, the goddess of wisdom and a woman, took Mentor's form and became a counselor and friend to Odysseus's son, Telemachus. Mentor protected and nurtured Telemachus while Odysseus was absent. She also took on the role of introducing him to those who could guide him as leaders should be guided (Bell, 1996; Bizzari, 1995). The mentoring process also has been cited in Sophocles's words: "The reasonable thing is to learn from those who can teach." Furthermore, records from the Renaissance period have shown that mentoring was a commonly accepted method of educating young persons (Wickman, 1997). Although the mentoring process can be seen throughout history, it is only in recent years that empirical research has been conducted on the effectiveness of this powerful strategy. It is even more recently that evidence has begun to accumulate showing the importance of mentoring to the development of women and individuals from minority groups. This chapter attempts to provide a brief overview of the past, present, and future of mentoring as a framework for the chapters that follow in this book.

The Past

The roots of the concept of mentoring are important and provide a framework for looking at the concept today. As one examines the story of Mentor in Homer's *The Odyssey*, several interesting points may be noted. First, I believe it is important to notice that the original "mentor" was a woman. This is relevant to our discussions of the development of mentoring as a strategy throughout history. From this original concept, one might assume either that mentors were generally women or that the form of mentor could be assumed by man or woman. In fact, throughout history, men traditionally have served as mentors and have utilized this powerful process far more than women to further their own careers and interests. As previously stated, it has been only in recent history that women have begun to recognize and benefit from mentoring.

Although the use of mentoring as a process for developing and furthering one's career and interests has been used primarily by men, it is not surprising that the original mentor figure was a woman. If one examines the roles that Mentor took in caring for Telemachus, it can be noted that Mentor (Athena) both protected and nurtured him as well as introduced him to individuals who could guide him as leaders should be guided. In today's language, Mentor provided both career functions (introducing him to leaders) and psychosocial functions (protection and nurturance) to her protégé (Kram, 1986). She used her nurturing and relational characteristics to care for him and to provide him with opportunities for psychosocial development while connecting him to persons who were in power and thus able to teach him to be a leader. Given the time in history, those individuals who were in power were probably male, and Mentor provided opportunities for Telemachus to network with those who were in better positions to help him develop as a leader (career skills).

In sum, the original concept of mentoring embodied both career and psychosocial functions, both of which are recognized today as essential components of successful mentoring relationships. The concepts of networking and multiple mentoring also were seen in the original conception of the mentoring process. Mentoring meant providing introductions and connections with individuals who were in power and who could further the career of the protégé. In addition, Mentor was not the only individual who was involved in furthering Telemachus's development. She introduced him to other leaders, who then also became mentors in their own rights.

From its original roots, mentoring developed into a strategy that was used primarily by men to further the protégé's career in business and industry. This development makes intuitive sense because, historically, men have been in senior positions and thus best able to mentor junior colleagues. Furthermore, until the relatively recent past, women were not encouraged to pursue careers but rather to choose traditional roles such as wife and mother. Therefore, mentoring developed as a strategy through which those in powerful positions groomed their protégés.

The Present

Traditional definitions of mentoring see the process as an intense interpersonal exchange between an experienced senior colleague (mentor) and a less experienced junior colleague (protégé) in which the mentor provides support, direction, and feedback regarding the protégé's career plans and personal development (Hall, 1976; Kram, 1985). Mentors also provide support to their protégés in an effort to remove organizational barriers, to assist protégés in negotiating the "system," and to provide protégés with opportunities for upward mobility (Kram, 1985).

More recently, researchers have identified three primary components of the mentoring process: career, psychosocial, and role modeling (Kram, 1986; Scandura & Ragins, 1993). Career functions are aimed at organizational advancement and include providing the protégé with sponsorship, exposure, coaching, protection, and challenging assignments. Psychosocial functions include efforts designed to foster the protégé's self-worth, competence, identity, and effectiveness through friendship, acceptance, and counseling. Role modeling has recently been identified as a separate factor associated with mentoring. Role modeling by the mentor allows the protégé to identify with the mentor and to emulate the desirable characteristics of the senior colleague.

It should be noted that often the terms *role model* and *mentor* are used interchangeably; however, recent research has shown that role modeling may be a factor associated with mentoring but by itself does not constitute a mentoring relationship. Examples of role models might include famous individuals who are seen as the best at their chosen professions, such as Michael Jordan, Janet Reno, and John Glenn. However, for a role model to be considered a mentor under the traditional definition, an intense interpersonal relationship must exist. Therefore, the role model may serve some of the same functions as a mentor without actually being a mentor.

The role-modeling function of mentoring is a critical factor. One reason why women may not have benefited as readily from the mentoring process in the past is a lack of female role models, particularly highly visible female role models with whom female protégés could readily identify. This has only recently begun to change as women have moved into more powerful and visible roles. The role-model factor has been even more absent for women of color and women who represent other minorities. Examples include Black role models, disabled female role models, and older female role models. This is not to suggest that role models did not previously exist among these groups; however, their visibility and the power of their respective positions have been limited in many instances. Therefore, protégés seeking to find role models with whom they could readily identify may have been faced with choosing between and among role models without power or visibility, such as relatives and friends, and male role models in positions of power. This absence of visible role models for both women and members of other underrepresented groups often results in those individuals compromising or not fully realizing their own potentials.

The lack of women, and in particular women of color, in the fields of science and some areas of business may be attributed in part to the lack of female role models with whom the protégé might identify. To point out the importance of role models with whom the individual might identify, consider the young Hispanic woman who wishes to be both a wife and mother and a professional scientist. If no female role models are available, the young woman may be faced with choosing a profession that she perceives as more consistent with being both a wife and mother and a professional or choosing a male mentor who does not provide her with opportunities to see how both roles may be balanced. If no role models are available, she may feel she needs to choose between the two roles, and her full potential may not be realized. In sum, women develop their careers and enter the workforce in different patterns than men and, therefore, may need a different type of mentoring than traditional male mentoring. The presence and availability of female role models may be a beginning in encouraging women and other individuals from underrepresented groups to look for and establish mentoring relationships.

In addition to identifying functions of the mentoring process, Kram (1983, 1985) identified four phases of the mentoring process. These phases begin with the initiation phase, which occurs within the first 6 to 12 months of the relationship. The mentoring relationship then becomes more intense during the cultivation phase, which may last anywhere from 2 to 5 years. Following the cultivation phase, the separation phase may begin and may last from 6 to 24 months. During this phase, the mentor and the protégé may begin both a structural and a psychological separation. Finally, the mentor and the protégé may enter the redefinition stage, during which the mentor and the protégé renegotiate their relationship from a mentorship to a more colleagial or peerlike relationship.

In addition, Kram (1983) suggested that the career function usually is the first to emerge in the mentoring relationship and that the psychosocial support becomes important later in the relationship or may be fulfilled through other nonmentor sources (Chao, Walz, & Gardner, 1992). This may be linked to the male definition of mentoring. The more task-oriented function, career, comes first and foremost in the mentoring relationship. The psychosocial support function is fulfilled either later as the relationship develops or through other sources.

This seems to imply that a lesser value or priority is placed on the more relational functions of mentorship, consistent with the traditional male model. It also may be one of the reasons why women traditionally have not benefited from the mentoring process to the same extent as men have. Whereas male mentoring relationships are characterized by acceptance of the hierarchy and task activity, females seem to prefer more psychosocial and emotional support in their organizational relationships. This support has been shown to be so important to women that they often rely on their peers for mentoring rather than looking further up in the organization to individuals in positions of power for a mentoring relationship (Kram & Isabella, 1985). As a consequence, women may fulfill their needs for psychosocial and emotional support from peer mentors at the expense of career growth and development available from influential and powerful mentors.

The discussion to this point has begun to highlight some of the benefits and barriers to mentoring in its present form. Research has shown that individuals with mentors receive more promotions

(Dreher & Ash, 1990), have higher incomes (Dreher & Ash, 1990), and report more career satisfaction (Turban & Dougherty, 1994) and mobility (Scandura, 1992) than those without mentors. Protégés also report reduced role stress and role conflict (Wilson & Elman, 1990).

Organizations, too, have realized the benefits of mentoring and have begun efforts to formalize the process as a sanctioned part of career development. In addition, many employees in today's workplace expect organizations to provide opportunities for them to fulfill their career and developmental needs (Aryee, Chay, & Chew, 1996). Some of the benefits that have been reported in the literature include relationships between mentoring and increased employee productivity (Silverhart, 1994), enhanced organizational commitment (Aryee et al., 1996), and lower levels of turnover (Viator, 1991). Mentoring also provides benefits to organizations because protégés are identified and groomed for management positions and employees become socialized to the companies' values through the mentoring process.

Finally, mentors receive benefits from mentoring their protégés. Mentors report increased status and greater internal satisfaction and fulfillment. Many mentors experience a sense of renewal and rejuvenation as well as benefiting from the creativity and energy of their protégés. Mentors also may benefit from the loyalty of their protégés as the protégés attain new levels of career advancement and the mentors may be recognized for their efforts as mentors by their organizations.

To this point, our discussion has been gleaned largely from mentoring in business and industry, which is not to suggest that mentoring efforts have not sprung up across disciplines. However, it has been only in the recent past that other organizations have begun to recognize and capitalize on the benefits of mentoring in both formal and informal situations. The increasing prevalence of mentoring was noted by Allen and Johnston (1997), who reported that more than 500 articles on mentoring were published in popular and academic publications in business and education in the past decade. Their report seems to suggest that mentoring is a powerful strategy that is receiving much attention in a variety of settings.

There is empirical evidence that suggests that mentoring as a prevention strategy has positive effects on young persons (Freedman, 1988). Mentors can help young people overcome personal and social barriers, expose them to new relationships and opportunities, and assist them in the development of skills. Mentoring programs have been developed in schools for at-risk students, gifted and talented students, and special education students. Intergenerational mentoring programs and peer mentoring programs also have been developed and implemented in public schools.

Mentoring has been recognized as a valuable tool in the development of teachers and has been used extensively as a part of teacher training (Martin, 1997). Higher education also has recognized the value of mentoring, and faculty often develop mentoring relationships with graduate, and to a lesser extent undergraduate, students. With the help of mentoring, students can become more deeply involved in the academic community and its diverse institutions. In addition, students learn the formal and informal structure of the institutions and of their respective career fields, and faculty mentors may provide feedback and serve as role models (Brown-Wright, Dubick, & Newman, 1997).

Community programs also have been developed that capitalize on the benefits of mentoring. Adopt-a-Grandparent Programs, Juvenile Justice and Delinquency Prevention Programs, and Big Brothers/Big Sisters Programs pair youth and adults or older persons. In this way, both the mentor and the protégé benefit from the interaction. Common outcomes of such programs include increased protégé self-esteem, decreased truancy, decreased delinquent behavior, increased academic achievement, and lower dropout rates.

In fact, mentoring just intuitively makes sense. Most of us can think back to personal memories of favorite teachers, coaches, neighbors, or community leaders who gave of their time and attention during critical periods in our lives. These individuals established interpersonal relationships with us that have affected who we are today.

Several barriers also exist to the establishment of effective mentoring relationships. These include limited availability of mentors, retention of mentors, inadequate mentor training and support, and interpersonal issues that may arise between mentors and protégés (Freedman, 1988). Additional barriers may exist related to mentoring opportunities for women and members of other underrepresented groups. Some of these barriers were mentioned previously, including lack of role models and mentors with whom individuals can identify, lack of women and members of underrepresented groups in positions of power to serve as mentors, and lack of recognition of the importance of mentoring for upward mobility.

Mentoring relationships can be divided into two categories: informal and formal. Informal mentoring involves the development of spontaneous relationships that occur without external involvement from the organization. These relationships are formed on the basis of the mutual agreement of mentor and protégé when the protégé proves himself or herself worthy of the attention provided by the mentor (Chao et al., 1992). These relationships are usually undefined, and no formal contract exists between the individuals. The time commitment to the mentoring relationships and the duration of the relationships are mutually negotiated and agreed on.

Formal mentorships are formally managed and sanctioned by the organization. Many organizations have mentoring programs in which mentors are paired with protégés in a number of ways, ranging from random assignment to matching based on personal interests and characteristics (Chao et al., 1992). Formal mentorships provide many of the benefits of informal mentoring relationships. However, because the pairings are artificially made, sometimes individuals who are chosen are incompatible, and, therefore, the mentoring relationship is unsuccessful. In addition, if the mentoring program is required, both mentor and protégé may not experience the same level of investment that otherwise might occur from a spontaneous, mutually agreed on relationship. Formal mentorships have the added advantage of allowing both parties to receive recognition by the organization for participating in the relationship, and cross-gender mentoring relationships may benefit from the organizational sanctioning of a relationship that might otherwise be misconstrued as having inappropriate sexual overtones.

Several alternative types of mentoring relationships have recently been proposed. These include peer mentoring, group mentoring, intergenerational mentoring, and subordinate mentoring. Models of multiple mentoring relationships also have been proposed as being the most beneficial because they allow the individual to benefit from a wide range of mentor ideas and experiences.

As societal needs and workplace demands continue to change, so does the nature of the mentoring relationships that are formed to meet these demands. Mentoring needs of women, people of color, people with disabilities, unemployed individuals, at-risk children and adults, older persons, and children with exceptional abilities are just a few of the areas that have been receiving attention recently both in the literature and in practice.

The Future

The future of mentoring will be determined not only by these changing needs but also through further study of the process itself. Researchers must continue to refine the definition of mentoring and how it differs from other behaviors such as coaching, networking, and counseling. The new types of mentoring relationships, including peer mentoring and group mentoring, must be researched to examine their effectiveness and unique contributions and barriers. The phases of mentoring need to be further defined and explored. Studies that examine the unique needs of groups such as women, people of color, and at-risk youth need to continue. From these investigations, new models of mentoring or modified mentoring programs may result.

In addition to investigating differences in needs of individuals for mentoring, it is imperative that studies integrate findings from mentoring studies across settings. As mentoring continues to receive more and more attention in educational, community, and counseling settings, similarities and differences among mentoring relationships in these settings may contribute to the continued refinement of this beneficial process.

Those of us in the counseling field have experienced mentoring in a variety of ways. School counselors have developed mentoring programs for at-risk children, gifted children, young women, and people of color, to name a few. These programs have been aimed at reducing dropout rates, increasing attendance and academic performance, and building self-esteem. They have included the use of several types of mentoring relationships as well as peer mentoring, intergenerational mentoring, formal mentoring, and informal mentoring. Additionally, school counselors have found themselves serving as mentors to individual students who seek them out.

Indirectly, school counselors may have been involved in the mentoring process themselves as protégés. More experienced school counselors, professors, and principals may serve as mentors to beginning school counselors. They also may find themselves involved in the development of mentoring partnerships in the community, pairing successful individuals with interested students, or other programs such as Big Brothers/Big Sisters. School counselors also may be indirectly involved or influenced by mentoring relationships occurring between student teachers, new teachers, and established teachers. In sum, school counselors may be participating in or may be responsible for a number of mentoring types of programs and relationships. It is therefore imperative that they are familiar with the benefits and barriers that may be associated with this process.

Community counselors are also exposed to mentoring relationships with increasing frequency. Experienced community counselors may serve as mentors to beginning counselors by providing support and supervision. Community counselors also may form and/or continue mentoring relationships with their counseling professors as they enter practice. They may serve as peer counselors to one another or as mentors to practicum and internship students. In addition, community counselors may develop and implement formal mentoring programs for clients, connecting potential mentors and protégés. These may include collaborative mentoring programs with schools, community organizations, and individuals. Finally, community counselors may serve as mentors to their clients. Although the topic of counselors serving as mentors for clients seems to create some ethical questions regarding boundaries and other ethical issues, the fact remains that many clients report viewing their counselors as important mentors. This is an issue that warrants further investigation among counselors across settings.

Counselors who work in employee assistance programs and career centers also may have direct experiences with mentoring in both formal and informal settings. This may be especially true as business and industry continue to respond to changes in the workforce. Issues such as downsizing, restructuring, and the increasing use of technology may have implications for the development of mentoring programs. Other areas, such as the unique needs of women, persons of color, persons with disabilities, displaced homemakers, and nontraditional-age students, also may be positively influenced by the development of informal and formal mentoring relationships.

Finally, counselor educators often serve as mentors to students as well as junior faculty and peers. They help students gain access to their profession and begin to identify themselves as professionals. These mentoring relationships may last well beyond the completion of the students' degrees and into the students' continued development in practice settings. Counselor educators also mentor beginning counselor educators as they progress toward tenure and promotion. They also may participate in mentoring faculty members from other disciplines in their own institutions. These may occur through the development of formal and informal mentoring relationships. Counselor educators may serve as peer mentors, providing support and consultation to colleagues. They also may assist students in the formation and establishment of peer mentoring programs. For example, 2nd-year students may serve as mentors for incoming students in a semistructured mentoring program facilitated by a faculty member.

In conclusion, mentoring is not a new concept. However, the nature of the process has changed considerably over time and will continue to evolve. As has already been highlighted, there are numerous areas ripe for exploration and application. The chapters that follow represent discussions of a variety of topics in which counseling and mentoring may have applications for one another. It is our hope that they will stimulate continuing dialogue and research on the synergy between counseling and mentoring.

References

Allen, J., & Johnston, K. (1997). Mentoring. *Context, 14*(7), 15.

Aryee, S., Chay, Y. W., & Chew, J. (1996). The motivation to mentor among managerial employees. *Group and Organization Management, 21,* 261–277.

Bell, C. R. (1996). *Managers as mentors: Building partnerships for learning.* San Francisco: Berrett Koehler.

Bizzari, J. (1995, Spring). Women: Role models, mentors, and careers. *Horizons,* 145–152.

Brown-Wright, D., Dubick, R., & Newman, I. (1997). Graduate assistant expectation and faculty perception: Implications for mentoring and training. *Journal of College Student Personnel, 38,* 410–415.

Chao, G. T., Walz, P. M., & Gardner, P. D. (1992). Formal and informal mentorships: A comparison on mentoring functions and contrast with non-mentored counterparts. *Personnel Psychology, 45,* 619–636.

Dreher, G. F., & Ash, R. A. (1990). A comparative study of mentoring among men and women in managerial, professional, and technical positions. *Journal of Applied Psychology, 75,* 539–546.

Freedman, M. (1988). *Partners in growth: Elder mentors and at-risk youth.* Philadelphia: Public/Private Ventures.

Hall, D. T. (1976). *Careers in organizations.* Glenview, IL: Scott, Foresman.

Homer. (1919). *The odyssey.* Cambridge, MA: Harvard University Press.

Kram, K. E. (1983). Phases of the mentor relationship. *Academy of Management Journal, 26,* 608–625.

Kram, K. E. (1985). *Mentoring at work: Developmental relationships in organizational life.* Glenview, IL: Scott, Foresman.

Kram, K. E. (1986). Mentoring in the workplace. In D. T. Hall (Ed.), *Career development in organizations* (pp. 160–201). San Francisco: Jossey-Bass.

Kram, K. E., & Isabella, L. A. (1985). Mentoring alternatives: The role of peer relationships in career development. *Academy of Management Journal, 28,* 110–132.

Martin, D. (1997). Mentoring in one's own classroom: An exploratory study of contexts. *Teacher and Teacher Education, 13,* 183–197.

Scandura, T. A. (1992). Mentorship and career mobility: An empirical investigation. *Journal of Organizational Behavior, 13,* 169–174.

Scandura, T. A., & Ragins, B. R. (1993). The effects of sex and gender role orientation on mentorship in male-dominated occupations. *Journal of Vocational Behavior, 43,* 251–265.

Silverhart, T. A. (1994, October). It works: Mentoring drives productivity higher. *Managers Magazine, 69,* 14–15.

Turban, D. B., & Dougherty, T. W. (1994). Role of protégé personality in receipt of mentoring and career success. *Academy of Management Journal, 37,* 688–702.

Viator, R. E. (1991). A study of mentor–protégé relationships in large public accounting firms. *Accounting Horizons, 5,* 20–30.

Wickman, F. (1997). *Mentoring.* New York: Irwin Professional Group.

Wilson, J. A., & Elman, N. S. (1990). Organizational benefits of mentoring. *Academy of Management Executive, 4,* 88–93.

CHAPTER

Men and Mentoring

By Valerie L. Schwiebert

*A*t first glance, one might intuitively assume that there is a strong connection between gender and the process of mentoring by the very fact that the term *mentoring* starts with the word *men*. In fact, mentoring has historically been a process developed and used by men primarily to benefit other men in climbing the corporate ladder (Ragins, 1989). Researchers have shown that mentoring is a crucial factor in upward organizational mobility and that far more men than women participate in these relationships. To understand the current state of mentoring and its implications for the counseling profession, it is important for us to understand the development of mentoring as a process. Therefore, it seems only logical that we begin our discussions with a chapter addressing the mentoring needs and strategies of men, the group that historically has had the greatest impact on the development of this process. This chapter explores the unique contributions of men to the development of mentoring as a process. Benefits and barriers that result from this male model of mentoring are explored. Differences and similarities between mentoring needs and styles of men and women are highlighted.

Men, particularly White men, have traditionally held positions of power and influence in the world of work. The concept of mentoring began as a developmental process by which a senior professional assisted a junior protégé in successfully negotiating the world of work and climbing the corporate ladder. It is important to note that mentoring was seen in terms of vocational progress and promotion. Although this book focuses on mentoring and its applications in the field of counseling, we must understand the historical development of the process that lies in the corporate world. This has implications for understanding how the process of mentoring developed as well as the particular benefits and liabilities of mentoring from a male perspective. Once the development of the mentoring process is understood, we can begin to evaluate its application to other groups of individuals and across settings.

White men have long held positions of power and influence in the corporate and business sectors. According to Dreher and Cox (1996), individuals are more likely to form developmental relationships with individuals whom they perceive as similar to themselves. Therefore, it follows that White men have greater access to powerful male (White) mentors and are more likely to benefit from the mentoring process than are their female counterparts or male counterparts of other races. The need to differentiate between all mentoring relationships and those formed by and with White male mentors is based on the fact that White male mentors have been shown to be particularly influential in affecting the career outcomes of their protégés.

Some examples of this influence include the fact that in several studies, female mentors were seen as less powerful than their male counterparts (Ragins & Sundstrom, 1989). Additionally, Erut and Mokros (1984) found that male students avoided selecting female mentors because they viewed the women as less powerful and of lower status than the men. Because of these factors and others, male mentors may be better able to confer organizational legitimacy on their protégés and to provide the resources and networking opportunities required for success (Ragins, 1989).

In the world of business, a significant proportion of these perceptions may be legitimate and may be based on power embedded in organizational position (Dreher & Cox, 1996). Fierman (1990) reported that of the 4,012 employees in 799 large U.S. companies, only 19 women were listed among those identified as the highest paid employees. Furthermore, *Business Week*'s review of corporate leaders reported that 99% of the chief executive officers of the largest U.S. companies were White men ("The Corporate Elite," 1991).

It is important to note that the position of White men in organizations may account for the main career support aspects of mentoring. There is evidence to suggest that the psychosocial functions as well as the role-model functions defined in the previous chapter may be better fulfilled by mentoring dyads consisting of same-gender and same-race individuals. For example, Jeruchim and Shapiro (1992) found that male mentors gave more instrumental assistance and sponsorship whereas female mentors gave more emotional support and personal advice. They attributed the lack of instrumental assistance provided by female mentors to the less powerful positions of women in organizations. However, women tend to be more relational than men and may benefit equally from mentoring that meets their psychosocial needs and provides emotional support.

Ragins (1989) reported that not only do male protégés receive different treatment from their mentors but they also seem to more effectively use their mentors. An example of the way in which male protégés seem to use their mentoring relationships more effectively than female protégés can be found in research related to termination of the mentoring relationship. Collins (1983) found that men may tend to actively seek a mentor, gain all that they can from him, and then move on to the next mentoring relationship. However, women reported having fewer mentors and were more likely to maintain these relationships past their usefulness. In fact, men older than 40 were likely to shift from the role of protégé to the role of mentor, whereas women were willing to remain in the role of protégé well past the age of 40. This difference may be due to the lack of fit between the needs of women and members of other underrepresented groups and the male mentoring strategies that have grown out of the White male power structure in organizations (Keyton & Kalbfleisch, 1993). The lack of fit also may account, in part, for the reasons why women and members of other underrepresented groups do not seek mentors and why White male mentors do not select women or members of underrepresented groups as protégés.

On the basis of the discussion so far, cross-gender mentoring may intuitively seem to be advantageous for mentoring women. Because White men are in positions of power and influence, it would seem that mentoring relationships in which the mentor is a White male and the protégé is a female would be most beneficial to the protégé. However, there are extensive studies that have documented the disadvantages of these types of mentoring relationships. First, there is a greater chance in cross-gender mentoring relationships for anxiety to develop regarding intimacy and physical attraction between mentor and protégé (Clawson & Kram, 1984). Second, the potential for public image problems to occur as a result of cross-gender mentoring relationships is another negative consequence of these types of relationships. Even when no romantic involvement is present, the mere perception by others may lead to negative consequences for mentor and protégé. The benefits and liabilities of cross-gender mentoring are addressed in detail later in this book.

Thus, what are the benefits of traditional mentoring relationships for both male mentors and protégés? Men tend to be socialized to strive for position and power and to be more task-oriented than women. Men also seem to recognize the importance of establishing mentoring relationships with other men in powerful positions as a means of achieving their goals of upward mobility in the world of work. Women, in contrast, tend to view competence as the only attribute necessary for success and may not recognize the importance of establishing mentoring relationships for personal and career success. Therefore, for men, identifying a male mentor in a powerful position provides the protégé with the opportunity for advancement as well as a male role model (Ragins, 1989).

Male protégés who form relationships with male mentors are more likely than female protégés to have similar career patterns and life experiences than their female counterparts. This allows the male protégés to benefit more directly from the mentoring experiences of their male mentors. For example, men tend to pursue an education and then enter a trade, career, or vocation. They continue on the path toward advancement as quickly as possible, without interruption. In contrast, women may delay education or a vocation or may interrupt a career in order to have children, marry, or establish a family life. The male mentor may be unable to identify with the female experience of juggling roles and varying career development, making him a more effective mentor for a male protégé than for a female protégé (Ragins, 1989).

Male protégés who form mentoring relationships with male mentors are also less likely than female protégés to experience either real or perceived sexual strain in their relationships. For example, a man who often works late with his male mentor probably would not experience the same type of office gossip, regardless of its validity, as a woman who stays late with the same male mentor. Furthermore, male protégés are less likely to be the recipients of unwanted sexual advances from their male mentors (Clawson & Kram, 1984).

Typical sex role stereotypes such as the woman being subservient to the man and needing to be protected, fathered, or cared for are also not as evident for male protégés with male mentors. Although male protégés may experience male mentors as paternalistic, the expectations of the male mentors tend to be related to pushing the male protégés to excel and are not related to protecting the protégés. The converse also may be true. That is, male protégés may not be expected to do everything exceptionally well because male–male mentoring relationships do not attract the same type of scrutiny because of their relative acceptance as the norm rather than as the exception for mentoring relationships.

Other benefits to male protégés include access to the many male social activities that are crucial to advancing within organizations. Male protégés may be invited to join weekly poker games, run with the other men at lunch, play golf, or stop at a local bar for a drink after work. These same activities would take on totally different social consequences if a male mentor were to invite a female protégé or if a female mentor were to invite a male protégé to social events outside of work. These social activities can be key opportunities for networking and making other connections that ultimately lead to advancement and can be of great benefit to male protégés in mentoring relationships with male mentors. These same social activities can assist male protégés in entering the "inner circle" of male power and influence within an organization that is often off-limits to female protégés who run into the so-called glass ceiling.

Male protégés also may benefit in subtle ways from mentoring relationships. For example, behaviors that are rewarded in male protégés, such as assertiveness and initiative, often are seen as socially inappropriate when displayed by female protégés. Male mentors may tend to encourage behaviors such as assertiveness in male protégés as a way to get ahead while either discouraging them in female protégés or not recognizing the potentially negative consequences of such behaviors for female protégés.

Male protégés are more likely to recognize the importance of seeking out mentoring relationships. Conversely, male mentors are more likely to recognize the importance of those same mentoring relationships and make special efforts to form these relationships with male protégés who show promise for achievement. In this way, the male mentor may benefit from the relationship through recognition of his mentoring efforts and the success of his protégé. He also may experience a feeling of generativity, a central task of midlife (Erikson, 1963).

Finally, male protégés and male mentors may benefit from similar communication styles and ways of relating to the world. The same problem-solving, task-oriented approach to life may help the protégé and the mentor connect more easily than cross-gender relationships that may require both parties to engage in an unfamiliar or uncomfortable approach. Cross-gender relationships may require women to learn more task-oriented approaches whereas men may need to learn more relational approaches. This can be frustrating to both parties, ultimately resulting in establishing a less successful mentoring relationship (Tannen, 1990).

There are also several disadvantages associated with traditionally male mentoring relationships. As previously discussed, male mentoring relationships are often very effective at providing career advancement and role modeling. However, these traditional approaches to mentoring may not meet the individual's needs for psychosocial support. Understanding and building relationships in the organization, emotional support, and nurturing may all be missing in the traditional male model of mentoring.

In addition, in fields that are not traditionally dominated by men, male protégés may have difficulty identifying male mentors and meeting their needs for male role models. This can be particularly difficult if the man in a nontraditionally male career continues to hold the same expectations for the mentoring relationship. He may find himself in a mentoring relationship that focuses on psychosocial support and does not provide the same opportunities for career advancement and role modeling that he may be expecting.

Another difficulty that may be experienced in male mentoring relationships occurs when male protégés are selected by male mentors on the basis of the potential mentors' assumptions that the male protégés must want and need mentors to get ahead. It may be difficult for potential male mentors to understand when younger male protégés choose not to participate in mentoring relationships. This may be particularly true as societal values change and older male mentors seek to establish traditional mentoring relationships with younger male protégés who may have differing values and priorities. Changing societal roles also may create differences between the career paths and other societal roles younger protégés may choose to undertake, creating distance between traditional male mentors and protégés. For example, more men are actively participating in their children's lives, and dual-career couples are making choices based on the needs of both partners. This may be an experience that is difficult for traditional male mentors to identify with and understand, ultimately affecting the mentoring relationship.

To this point, we have discussed the evolution of mentoring from an organizational–career perspective. The question now becomes, how is the male model of mentoring important to the field of counseling? What implications, if any, does this model have for counselors and clients in a variety of settings? The answers to these questions form the rest of the discussion in this chapter.

Counselors must understand the evolution of the process of mentoring from its male and organizational roots if they are to effectively use the process to their own benefit as well as to the benefit of their clients. Traditional mentoring models, based on the male model, do not provide clients or counselors with a comprehensive model of mentoring. An analogy may be drawn between the counseling process and the mentoring process. In the counseling process, the counselor begins by establishing rapport and building a relationship with the client. At the same time, the counselor is exploring the problem. As rapport is established and the problem understood, the process then moves into the goal-setting and solution-building phase. The counseling process is not fully effective if no rapport exists between client and counselor. If the client does not trust the counselor, it is unlikely that the real problem will be addressed or that effective solutions will result. Conversely, if there is great rapport and no problem solving or solution building, then the client does not receive the maximum therapeutic benefit.

Likewise, the traditional mentoring process is not as beneficial to either the mentor or the protégé when the focus of the process is only on career advancement. Maximum benefit may be attained from the mentoring relationship when efforts are made by both male and female mentors and protégés to focus on career advancement as well as psychosocial support. Because counselors and counselor educators both participate in mentoring relationships and use mentoring strategies to work with clients, it would seem that developing and implementing mentoring strategies and programs that incorporate both aspects of the mentoring process would be most beneficial. Unfortunately, in practice, many mentoring programs and relationships continue to be developed and implemented on the basis of the traditional male model of mentoring, resulting in a focus on only the career advancement aspects of the mentoring process.

An example of the entrenchment of the male model of mentoring that directly impacts the counseling profession can be seen in the academic training of counselors. Only recently have women begun to move into administrative positions in counselor training programs. For many years, male counselor educators have held the power positions in these programs, such as faculty chair, department head, and dean. Not only have men held the power positions, but female faculty members have been hard to find. Therefore, many female counseling students did not have the benefit of forming mentoring relationships during their counselor training programs, or they formed mentoring relationships with male mentors. This is interesting given the large numbers of female counseling students and the relative lack of potential female counselor educator mentors.

Male students, in contrast, had access to a variety of male mentors, which provided them with the opportunity to choose among the available male mentors. This allowed the male students to form relationships with mentors with whom they could identify and who also could serve as male role models. The male mentors were then able to assist the male protégés from these positions of relative power. This access to male mentors in powerful positions allowed many of the male counseling students to enter into positions and networks that could eventually lead them to the same positions of power, thus perpetuating the male-dominated system.

An example of how the traditional male system of mentoring worked to the disadvantage of a female doctoral student and to the advantage of a male doctoral student follows and is based on the true experiences of two counseling students. A female student applied to a doctoral program in counseling at the same time as her male friend. This program was one of the top counselor education programs in the country and at that time employed only 2 women and approximately 11 men. The women were assistant professors. The female counseling student, who had applied to the doctoral program, was interviewed by a male counseling professor. He told the female student that because women often get pregnant and do not finish doctoral programs, she should obtain her educational specialist degree first and then work toward her doctorate if she still felt that was an option for her. He explained that although her application materials were outstanding, he felt that women did not have the same commitment to finishing their dissertations and doctoral programs because family commitments were more important than their career aspirations. The male student interviewed with the same male faculty member. He was told that even though his application materials were not particularly strong, with the proper guidance, he would do fine in his doctoral program. The educational specialist degree was never discussed as an option for him.

The female student did register for and complete the educational specialist degree. She formed a mentoring relationship with one of the female professors. Through this mentoring relationship, she was encouraged to continue in the doctoral program. Her mentor also served as a sponsor, coach, supporter, and role model. The female student graduated with her doctorate in counselor education and went on to become a practicing counselor and faculty member. The male student entered into a mentoring relationship with the male professor who had interviewed him. The professor had "picked him." The male professor had high aspirations for the male doctoral student and devoted a great deal of effort to the mentoring relationship. The male doctoral student felt obligated to live up to the expectations of his mentor and to finish his program despite the fact that he really felt he did not want to be a counselor. He finally did graduate and currently works in a field completely unrelated to the counseling profession.

Although this example is certainly not the experience of most counselor educators or counseling students, it highlights a number of issues related to the impact that mentoring may have on potential counselors and counselor educators. The traditional male model of mentoring that stresses achievement and career advancement did compel the male student to complete his doctoral program in counseling. However, the lack of psychosocial support and the lack of a relational component in the mentoring process did not serve him well. In fact, if he had been given the opportunity to explore his feelings, values, and beliefs, he may have left the program in the early stages and gone on to pursue his current career. This would have saved him time, money, and personal struggle.

His mentor was operating from a traditional male system of mentoring that he had probably experienced as a young counseling student and from which he had greatly benefited. He was trying to use this same mentoring approach to benefit his protégé. He was merely trying to further the career of the young doctoral student. The mentoring model that he knew did not include the psychosocial component in addition to the career advancement component. He saw the young doctoral student's struggles as part of the developmental process of becoming a counseling professional and his role as to push him in directions that would further the protégé's counseling career. In addition, it is interesting to note that the mentor is an outstanding counselor and never would have entered into a counseling relationship without focusing on building rapport as well as developing and taking action.

The male professor's interaction with the female doctoral student also was based on a male model of mentoring. Although some would argue that this was a blatantly sexist interaction, it also may be interpreted within the framework of his model of mentoring. To

21

the male professor, the female student's best opportunities for career development would be to undertake the first option, educational specialist, to ensure that she received an advanced degree in counseling if she were unable to complete her doctoral work because of family commitments. He was unable to explore options with her that may have allowed her to consider both family obligations and doctoral work. This may have been due to his experience as a man in the counseling and academic professions. If he had been a woman, he may have been able to help the female student to find ways to balance her family commitments and doctoral work.

Other examples of the benefits and limitations of the traditional male model of mentoring can be seen in the development of mentoring programs in counseling settings. Schools, community counseling programs, college and university counseling programs, and employee assistance programs all utilize the mentoring concept in some form. The traditional model that emphasizes career advancement is important in developing mentoring programs and in working with clients in individual settings. High school counselors may develop mentoring programs that focus on pairing students with successful professionals in the community who can motivate the students to pursue their chosen careers. Individual career counselors may work with clients who feel cheated because they may have wanted a mentor and never found one. If the career counselor recognizes that the client is operating from a more traditional view of mentoring, the counselor can help the client expand that model to include both career and psychosocial aspects of mentoring. In this way, the client may be able to identify individuals who have served as mentors yet who have never been labeled as such because of the limited definition the client held of mentor. It may also be helpful for the career counselor to explore with the client this traditional view of the mentoring role to ascertain if the client is somehow waiting for someone to take control of his or her career so that he or she can advance (Burlew, 1991).

In conclusion, it is important to understand the evolution of the concept of mentoring. This traditional view of mentoring grows out of the White man's experience in corporate America. The purpose of this type of mentoring is to further the career advancement of the individual and is largely based on a male model. This model has both advantages and limitations. Because mentoring and mentoring programs are common in the counseling profession, understanding the evolution of this model of mentoring and its impact on the counseling profession is important if counselors are to maximize the benefits of mentoring for themselves and their clients. The following chapters explore the expansion of the concept of mentoring to include role modeling, career advancement, and psychosocial functions as well as issues that affect the mentoring process, such as mentoring for women, multicultural issues, professional development in counseling, and professional issues.

References

Burlew, L. (1991). Multiple mentor model: A conceptual framework. *Journal of Career Development, 17,* 213–221.

Clawson, J. G., & Kram, K. E. (1984). Managing cross-gender mentoring. *Business Horizons, 27,* 22–32.

Collins, N. W. (1983). *Professional women and their mentors.* Englewood Cliffs, NJ: Prentice Hall.

The corporate elite. (1991, November 25). *Business Week,* (3241), 185–214.

Dreher, G. F., & Cox, T. H. (1996). Race, gender, and opportunity: A study of compensation attainment and the establishment of mentoring relationships. *Journal of Applied Psychology, 81,* 297–308.

Erikson, E. (1963). *Childhood and society.* New York: Norton.

Erut, S., & Mokros, J. R. (1984). Professors as models and mentors for college students. *American Educational Research Journal, 21,* 399–417.

Fierman, J. (1990, July 30). Why women still don't hit the top. *Fortune, 122,* 40–42, 46, 50, 54, 58, 62.

Jeruchim, J., & Shapiro, P. (1992). *Women, mentors and success.* New York: Fawcett Columbine.

Keyton, J., & Kalbfleisch, P. J. (1993, April). *Building a normative model of women's mentoring relationships.* Paper presented at the Joint Meeting of the Southern States Communication Association and the Central States Communication Association, Lexington, KY.

Ragins, B. R. (1989). Barriers to mentoring: The female manager's dilemma. *Human Relations, 42,* 1–22.

Ragins, B. R., & Sundstrom, E. (1989). Gender and power in organizations: A longitudinal perspective. *Psychological Bulletin, 105,* 51–88.

Tannen, D. (1990). *You just don't understand: Women and men in conversations.* New York: Morrow.

CHAPTER

Cross-Gender Mentoring

By Catherine Y. Chang and Valerie L. Schwiebert

*T*raditionally, the mentoring relationship has been recognized as an important aspect for the career and personal development of men. However, recently, the literature has begun to acknowledge that mentoring is equally important for the career success of women (Hunt & Michael, 1983; Ragins & Cotton, 1993) and that women are more likely than men to be involved in cross-gender mentoring relationships. Mentoring relationships are important for both the female protégé and the female mentor. The purpose of this chapter is to provide a description of cross-gender mentoring and a review of literature pertaining to cross-gender mentoring. In addition, the barriers to and potential benefits of cross-gender mentoring are discussed and strategies for fostering successful cross-gender mentoring relationships are proposed.

Description of Cross-Gender Mentoring

Although the majority of the literature and research on mentorship has focused on male-mentor/male-protégé relationships, the gender-based typology of mentor–protégé relationships demonstrates that two of the four typologies involve cross-gender mentor relationships and one involves all-female relationships (Shapiro, Haseltine, & Rowe, 1978). Shapiro et al. proposed four types of mentoring relationships, explained as a four-cell model. Cell 1 of Shapiro et al.'s typology focuses on men who have male mentors. Cell 2 focuses on male mentors with female protégés, Cell 3 emphasizes female mentors with male protégés, and Cell 4 accentuates female mentors with female protégés (Shapiro et al., 1978).

The majority of cross-gender mentor relationships involve male mentors with female protégés. This is largely due to a scarcity of female mentors in business, academia, and the professions (Hunt & Michael, 1983; Ragins & McFarlin, 1990) and the fact that most mentors are men (Scott, 1989). Scott suggested that there are more male mentors than female mentors because men occupy more of the higher level positions. There is some evidence that suggests that one must be at a certain stage in one's career development in order to become a mentor. The lack of women in advanced positions reduces the pool of potential female mentors (Bogat & Redner, 1985).

Scott (1989) also indicated that, traditionally, girls do not participate in team sports as much as boys do and, thus, are less likely to learn the politics of "team play." Therefore, professional women may not know how to mentor or may feel less competent to mentor. In addition, women tend to be more reluctant than men to become mentors (Scott, 1989).

Conversely, Ragins and Cotton (1993) found that women expressed equivalent intentions to mentor as men, although women anticipated more potential drawbacks and negative aspects of assuming a mentoring role. Women anticipated greater risks from becoming a mentor than men did, reported having less available time to be a mentor, and stated that they lacked the qualifications to be a mentor. In addition to anticipating greater drawbacks and risks, women may be less likely to serve as mentors because they did not have mentors; therefore, women lack the role modeling necessary to become mentors (Ragins & Cotton, 1993).

Men have a larger pool of available protégés than women. Whereas men are likely to have both men and women for protégés, women tend to have primarily female protégés. Male students were found to avoid selecting female faculty mentors because they viewed the female faculty as having less power and status than the male faculty (Erkut & Mokros, 1984). In addition, male mentors were perceived as role models for both male and female protégés, whereas female mentors were perceived as role models by primarily female protégés (Ragins & McFarlin, 1990).

Although women continue to advance professionally, the research shows that both male and female protégés are more likely to have male mentors (Feist-Price, 1994). Because of the scarcity of female mentors, the lack of women in advanced positions, and the perception that men have more power than women, cross-gender mentoring relationships are more prevalent among women than men (Ragins & McFarlin, 1990). Therefore, the typical cross-gender typology is that of a male mentor and a female protégé (Hunt & Michael, 1983).

A Review of Cross-Gender Mentoring Literature

Cross-gender mentoring has brought about considerable controversy (Schwiebert, Deck, Bradshaw, Scott, & Harper, 1998). The importance and benefits of mentoring have been well documented; however, it has been noted that differences, such as gender, between mentor and protégé may cause potential problems (Baugh, Lankau, & Scandura, 1996; Clawson & Kram, 1984). McCormick (1991) reported a high rate of success in mentoring relationships when both mentor and protégé were male, whereas the failure rate was higher when the mentoring relationship involved women. Goldstein's (1979) research study on same-gender and cross-gender adviser pairs indicated that the same-gender pairs were more productive than the cross-gender pairs in terms of early career publications. These differences in success between same-gender and cross-gender mentoring relationships may be due to the lack of fit of the male model of mentoring.

Noe (1988) studied successful assigned mentoring relationships and discovered that cross-gender mentoring relationships reported that these protégés used the mentorship more effectively than did the protégés matched with same-sex mentors. In addition, Noe found that female protégés used the mentorship more effectively than male protégés did. He hypothesized that women may be more highly motivated to use their mentors because of the general lack of mentors for women (Noe, 1988).

Although female protégés may use cross-gender mentorships more effectively than male protégés do, female protégés are at a disadvantage when compared with their male counterparts. Male mentors are inclined to select male protégés, and some men may hold negative attitudes toward women's competencies (Bogat & Redner, 1985). In addition, female protégés are more likely to experience overprotectiveness, greater social distance, and general discomfort in a male-mentored relationship than are male protégés. Female protégés may be more prone to emotional ties with their male mentors than are male protégés (Hunt & Michael, 1983).

Sex role expectations may impact the cross-gender mentoring relationship. Sex role expectations may lead protégés to perceive women as having less power than men, and conversely, female mentors may be perceived as providing more nurturance and social support than male mentors (Ragins & McFarlin, 1990). Ragins and McFarlin found that cross-gender protégés were less likely than same-gender protégés to report engaging in afterwork social activities with their mentors. To the extent that afterwork socializing is essential for networking and enhancing the cohesiveness of the mentoring relationship, cross-gender protégés face greater restrictions in developing the mentoring relationship than do same-gender protégés.

Differences between cross-gender and same-gender mentoring relationships also were found for role modeling. Same-gender mentoring pairs were more likely than cross-gender mentoring pairs to report that their mentors served as role models (Ragins & McFarlin, 1990). By observing their mentors, protégés may vicariously learn strategies for career and personal advancement and development. Cross-gender protégés face greater limitations to vicarious learning because of the lack of role modeling.

Although the existing mentorship theory suggests that gender influences the development of the mentoring relationship (Hunt & Michael, 1983), Scandura and Ragins (1993) have contended that research in this area reveals weak gender effects. Turban and Dougherty's (1994) study that examined protégé personality and the receipt of mentoring and career success found that protégé gender was not related to initiation of mentoring or mentoring received. Alleman, Cochran, Doverspire, and Newman (1984) found that mentors in cross-gender mentoring relationships did not behave differently from mentors in same-gender mentoring relationships.

Gender differences in cross-gender mentoring relationships may be overly simplistic, and the use of gender role orientation may be more appropriate for understanding the dynamics of mentoring relationships. Gender role orientation was found to be a stronger predictor of career development and psychosocial mentorship functions than biological sex; however, gender role orientation was unrelated to role-modeling function (Scandura & Ragins, 1993). Regardless of whether gender or gender role socialization has a greater influence on the cross-gender mentoring relationship, it is apparent that cross-gender mentoring relationships have certain limitations. In the next section, limitations to cross-gender mentoring relationships are discussed.

Barriers to Cross-Gender Mentoring Relationships

Cross-gender mentoring relationships may raise additional issues and complexities that are absent in same-gender mentoring relationships (Clawson & Kram, 1984). Clawson and Kram conceptualized cross-gender mentoring within a developmental dilemma in which the mentor and the protégé must manage both the internal and external relationships. The mentor and the protégé must manage the closeness and distance in the internal relationship as well as in the external relationship, the perceptions of the mentoring relationship by outsiders.

Kram (1985) identified five major barriers to cross-gender relationships that occur in the two sets of mentor roles, psychosocial and career development. Psychosocial roles that include the interpersonal aspects of mentoring may be influenced by sexual concerns and the restriction of identification in cross-gender mentoring relationships. Restriction of identification occurs when the protégé perceives the mentor as unable to fully understand his or her experience because of the differing experiences between the mentor and the protégé that are based on gender.

According to Kram (1985), specific barriers to cross-gender relationships include collusion in stereotypical roles, limitations of role modeling, intimacy and sexuality concerns, public scrutiny, and peer resentment. Collusion in stereotypical roles refers to the tendency of men and women to assume stereotypical roles in relating to each other at work when they are unsure of their roles. These roles are defined by assumptions and expectations about what is appropriate behavior for each gender. Stereotypical roles may reduce female competency and autonomy while accentuating the dominant role of the male. In addition, behaviors that are socially desirable and acceptable for men are not necessarily acceptable for women. Assertiveness and competitiveness are only a few examples of such behaviors. Stereotypical roles may distort and hinder the career development and psychosocial roles of the mentoring relationship (Clawson & Kram, 1984). Furthermore, assumption of stereotypical roles may lead to differences in male mentors' expectations for female protégés compared with their male counterparts regarding performance, competence, potential, and ability.

The second barrier to cross-gender mentoring is limitations for role modeling. Role modeling involves both interaction and identification. In cross-gender mentoring relationships, appropriate role modeling may be lacking because of a lack of identification with the opposite-sex mentor. A female protégé may be unable to identify with her male mentor in matters concerning work and home conflicts and issues related to child care. For example, a male mentor may not be able to empathize with a female protégé's struggles to balance her roles as wife, mother, homemaker, and professional. Not only may the male mentor not be able to empathize with the female protégé, but he may not understand or value her struggles to maintain a balance in all of these areas, nor is he able to model ways in which she might more easily manage these struggles. Similarly, a female mentor may be unable to empathize with a male protégé's need to live up to stereotypic role expectations such as being the breadwinner. Their relationship may be further complicated if he perceives the role of men to be breadwinners and the role of women to be homemakers because the female mentor may represent a direct contradiction to those traditional roles.

The risk of intimacy and sexual concerns are frequently mentioned as risks to cross-gender mentoring (Beck, 1989). The potential for sexual relationships can be threatening to men and women who work together. Concerns about increasing levels of intimacy can create tension and anxiety for both men and women. In addition, these sexual concerns may lead members of cross-gender relationships to restrict the friendship role, which involves trust, support, and intimacy. This restriction in the mentoring relationship may reduce the effectiveness of the mentoring relationship.

As a result of this concern about intimacy and sexual relationships, cross-gender mentoring pairs may avoid the frequency of interactions that same-gender mentoring pairs commonly engage in, thus hindering the development of the mentoring relationship. Another strategy that may be used by members of cross-gender mentoring relationships is the mentor assumes a parental role (Ragins & McFarlin, 1990). The parental role is viewed as asexual in nature, thereby reducing the possibility of the development of a sexual relationship. In this way, sexual tension may be lessened for both mentor and protégé. This barrier to cross-gender mentoring is considered especially problematic for male mentors with female protégés. However, with growing recognition of sexual harassment issues in the workplace, more female mentors have begun to express concerns related to cross-gender mentoring with male protégés.

Concerns regarding intimacy and sexual relationships in cross-gender mentoring relationships also may make female protégés less likely to approach male mentors. The female protégé may fear that her attempts to initiate a relationship may be misconstrued as a sexual approach by either the mentor or others in the organization (Ragins, 1989). In addition, research suggests that male mentors view approaches by potential male protégés more favorably than approaches by potential female protégés.

Public scrutiny and suspicion are also more likely to occur with cross-gender mentoring relationships. Even in the absence of actual sexual involvement, the rarity of cross-gender relationships makes them subject to greater public scrutiny, office gossip, and discrediting sexual innuendos. Public scrutiny impacts both perception and behavior. Because of increased public scrutiny, members of cross-gender mentoring relationships may choose to avoid one-on-one interaction behind closed doors and contact after work hours, as well as to restrict their friendship. Additionally, female protégés may avoid contact with their male mentors in informal settings such as golf clubs, lunches, running groups, and meetings at the gym. This restriction of the mentoring relationship denies female protégés access to networking and other social activities that may positively impact career development and enhancement.

The final barrier to cross-gender mentoring relationships, according to Kram (1985), involves peer resentment. Peer resentment is most prevalent with male mentors and female protégés working in a predominantly male group. The female protégés may be seen as receiving special attention because they receive mentoring from their male superiors. Again, this special attention may be seen as sexual in nature, resulting in office gossip and discrediting sexual innuendos. This may lead some female protégés to look to peer relationships for mentoring. One problem with this approach is that peers usually have less power and influence than mentors and may be less able to promote advancement in organizations.

Each of these five barriers is further influenced by individual and organizational factors. For example, the literature focuses on intimacy concerns that may occur between male and female mentor–protégé pairs. This assumes a heterosexual orientation. Gay, lesbian, and bisexual individuals may not experience the same barriers to cross-gender mentoring that heterosexual individuals experience. However, they may experience different barriers in these relationships, which have not been explored in the literature to date (Gelberg & Chojnacki, 1996).

With proper precautions, communication, and planning, each of the barriers to cross-gender mentoring relationships can be circumvented (Kram, 1985). Fostering a successful cross-gender mentoring relationship is discussed below, following a look at the benefits of cross-gender mentoring relationships.

Benefits of Cross-Gender Mentoring Relationships

Although the majority of benefits of mentoring relationships are based on same-sex mentoring relationships, and more specifically, male mentors and male protégés, they can be generalized to cross-gender mentoring relationships. Mentoring relationships can be mutually beneficial to the mentors, the protégés, and the organizations (Brown-Wright, Dubick, & Newman, 1997; Heimann & Pittenger, 1996; Kartje, 1996).

Mentoring can provide both career and psychosocial benefits for protégés (Noe, 1988). For protégés, mentoring has been linked to positive career choice, retention, promotion, and advancement; career satisfaction and success; income level; and a reduction in protégés' role stress (Baugh et al., 1996; Collins, Kamya, & Tourse, 1997). Mentor behaviors that can facilitate the career advancement of their protégés include nominating their protégés for projects and promotions, providing the protégés with assignments that increase visibility and exposure, sharing ideas, providing feedback and suggestions, and providing challenging work assignments.

Mentoring also enhances protégés' psychosocial functions, which include sense of competence, increased confidence in their ability, socialization into the organization, identity development, and work-role effectiveness (Brown-Wright et al., 1997; Graham, 1994; Noe, 1988). Mentors can enhance their protégés' psychosocial functioning by serving as role models of appropriate attitudes, values, and behaviors for the protégés. Thus, they convey unconditional positive regard, provide a forum in which the protégés are encouraged to talk openly about anxieties and fears, and interact informally with the protégés at work (Noe, 1988).

Female protégés may benefit from cross-gender mentoring relationships because male mentors may provide them with access to positions of advancement not previously available to women. Male mentors in positions of power can assist female protégés through sponsorship, support, encouragement, and access to important organizational networks. Male mentors also may serve as role models for female protégés.

Mentoring is mutually beneficial for the mentors. While protégés receive advice, coaching, support, and counsel in matters related to vocational and psychosocial development, mentors are provided with the opportunity to assist other individuals and to use their skills and knowledge (Burke, McKeen, & McKenna, 1990; Kartje, 1996). Mentors also may benefit from career advancements due to their mentoring relationship. As mentors work with protégés, they obtain new perspectives and insight into their work that could lead to career advancements. In addition, mentors may benefit from the mentoring relationship by being reminded of what it was like to be new and by having an opportunity to review and reappraise their own professional practice (Graham, 1994). Male mentors who are committed to the advancement of all individuals may feel a sense of satisfaction when they are able to help female protégés break gender barriers. In addition, as organizations are required by law to demonstrate diversity among their ranks, male mentors who sponsor competent female protégés may be looked on favorably as advancing the organization's agenda.

Organizations also can benefit from mentoring relationships because future leaders are prepared and individuals who are mentored display greater satisfaction and commitment to their organizations (Burke et al., 1990). Mentoring relationships can enhance team-building, which results in further team projects and may promote retention of workers (Graham, 1994).

Fostering a Successful Cross-Gender Mentoring Relationship

Despite the additional challenges to cross-gender mentorships, cross-gender mentoring relationships can be beneficial to the mentor, the protégé, and the organization. The failure of cross-gender mentoring relationships may be largely due to personal and organizational barriers (McCormick, 1991). To foster a successful cross-gender mentorship, one must consider the role of the mentor, the protégé, and the organization.

A successful cross-gender mentoring relationship calls for an increased level of maturity on the part of the mentor to cope with the possibility of sexual relationships (Hunt & Michael, 1983). In cross-gender mentoring relationships, both parties must effectively communicate the mentoring goals (Feist-Price, 1994) as well as define the boundary between appropriate levels of intimacy and romantic involvement (Clawson & Kram, 1984). Effective mentoring relationships require that mentors have a basic understanding of the role of mentors and the rationale behind mentoring (Brown-Wright et al., 1997).

Many of the characteristics that foster cross-gender mentoring relationships also encourage closer intimate relationships; therefore, both mentors and protégés must be aware of the dangers. Clawson and Kram (1984) identified seven aspects that they considered to be developmental dilemmas that represent characteristics of effective mentoring relationships as well as characteristics in budding romantic relationships. The dilemmas include (a) respect and admiration for the mentor, (b) trust in the mentor's consistent concern for the well-being of the protégé, (c) an informal style between mentor and protégé, (d) openness between mentor and protégé, (e) role complementarity, (e) frequent interactions, and (f) work that may lead to the mentor and the protégé adjusting their personal schedules to complete tasks.

For mentors and protégés to maintain platonic, professional relationships, Clawson and Kram (1984) suggested that both mentors and protégés assess positive and negative traits of their partner. Mentors and protégés may balance their attraction to cross-gender partners by focusing on their partner's shortcomings.

Maintaining an informal style is an important part of building an effective mentoring relationship; however, informality may lead to intimacy, if unchecked. It is suggested that mentors and protégés keep to first names only and that they not use pet names or terms of endearment. In addition, physical distance should be maintained. Touching, brushing up against a partner, and sitting close to the other should be avoided (Clawson & Kram, 1984).

Open communication also can be seen as enhancing and detrimental to the mentoring relationship. Clawson and Kram (1984) suggested that feelings of intimacy should not be expressed to the other. They recommended that one find someone else to talk to about these intimate feelings. In addition, they distinguished personal matters from private matters. Personal matters involve personal ways of coping with work and events at home that affect job performance, whereas private matters involve discussing one's fantasies and feelings of attraction. Personal matters are appropriate for discussion in a cross-gender platonic, professional mentoring relationship, whereas private matters are not. Clawson and Kram also recommended limiting the frequency of meeting between mentor and protégé, especially after work hours, and changing one's personal schedule so that mentor and protégé are not alone under stressful conditions.

Other strategies that may be used to diffuse sexual issues between mentor and protégé in a cross-gender mentoring relationship include getting to know your partner's family and/or spouse, talking about your mentor to your spouse or significant other, and confronting the issue in a straightforward manner if it arises. The use of immediacy may assist both mentor and protégé in focusing on the benefits of a working relationship and not confusing those with a romantic relationship. The mentor also should be aware of possible sexual issues and avoid sexual joking and innuendos or comments about the protégé's appearance. The mentor needs to be aware of public scrutiny and should try to reduce even the appearance of sexual intimacy by the use of such strategies as leaving the door open when talking with the protégé, inviting a third party along or going in groups when meeting for drinks or dinner, and avoiding situations such as inviting the protégé to one's home or hotel room.

Institutions, too, may assist mentors and protégés in cross-gender mentoring relationships by developing clear conflict-of-interest policies that clarify appropriate relationships and establish sexual harassment guidelines and policies. Institutions also may develop formal mentoring programs that involve cross-gender mentor pairs. These programs should include activities and opportunities for mentoring that are sanctioned by the institutions and therefore may lessen issues related to sexual intimacy both real and perceived. Organizations also can help to foster cross-gender mentoring relationships by securing cooperation from all members of the organizations and by systematically evaluating the mentoring relationships (Feist-Price, 1994; Redmond, 1990). Cross-gender mentoring programs are more likely to succeed and people are more cooperative if all members of the organizations understand the rationale behind the programs. Through structured ongoing evaluations, organizations can monitor and improve their cross-gender mentoring programs.

To increase the comfort level of interaction between cross-gender mentoring relationships, institutions can develop more sex-neutral activities and sites where interactions can occur naturally and comfortably in a sanctioned environment (McCormick, 1991) and without the hint of an inappropriate intimate relationship. At the opposite end of the risk of intimacy is the risk of distance. Mentors and protégés can get so caught up in maintaining a platonic, professional mentoring relationship that they maintain a distant relationship. Unnecessarily distant mentoring relationships can reduce the benefits of mentoring. Clawson and Kram (1984) suggested that mentors systematically assess themselves, their protégés, and the mentor–protégé relationship to determine the closeness of the relationship and then consider whether something should be done about the distance in the mentoring relationship. Both mentors and protégés are responsible for finding and establishing an appropriate balance of intimacy and distance that fosters learning, growth, and productivity; however, mentors, having more experience and power, must take the initiative and responsibility for managing these relationships.

An analogy between counselor and client may be helpful to consider. Counseling is a very intimate process, yet it is not sexual in nature. Boundaries must be established that allow the client to grow and learn yet prevent the development of an inappropriate sexual relationship. The same types of boundaries may be established in cross-gender mentoring relationships that allow an intimate relationship to exist without a sexual component. The counselor is responsible for maintaining the client's best interest in the counseling relationship. The same responsibility is assigned to the mentor, as mentioned previously, in the mentoring relationship.

Counselors and counselor educators serving as mentors in cross-gender mentoring relationships may use the situation as an opportunity to model and teach the importance of maintaining appropriate and professional boundaries while allowing for the development of necessary intimacy in the relationships. Mentors may even wish to discuss with their protégés the parallels between mentoring relationships and counseling relationships. Of course, it is important for mentors to point out differences that exist between the two situations as well. For example, the limitations of confidentiality in a mentoring relationship may be different than those in a counseling relationship. Other differences also should be highlighted, including the prohibition of dual-role relationships in the counseling process and the existence of dual-role relationships in the counselor education setting, for example.

Counselors and counselor educators who serve as mentors must also be careful to distinguish between the roles of counselor and mentor. This may be an area that is difficult to distinguish. Consultation with other professionals as well as the use of immediacy between protégé and counselor may help clarify differences between the two roles and distinguish between what is and what is not appropriate for the mentoring relationship.

In addition to considering the relationship between mentor and protégé, cross-gender mentoring relationships must consider public image. Mentor and protégé must be cognizant of their public image. A close mentoring relationship may lead to allegations of favoritism and accusations of intimate relationships, which can lead to demoralization and loss of respect for the mentor. Furthermore, these allegations, whether founded or not, may have negative consequences for the protégé.

Clawson and Kram (1984) provided the following suggestions for managing perceptions of intimacy, which include making sure that others in the organization become familiar with and witness the work of the protégés. They also suggested avoiding long after-hours meetings and scheduling meetings in advance. In addition, the same language and tone of voice should be used with protégés as with other colleagues. Pet expressions, nicknames, and inside jokes may suggest to others that there is something special going on between the mentor and the protégé.

A case example of a successful cross-gender mentoring relationship follows. A female counselor educator with 3 years of university teaching experience moved to a new institution. At this institution, she was immediately placed into an orientation and "mentoring" program. She was not given a choice regarding participation nor asked for any input regarding her needs or preferences for a mentor. Instead, another female instructor was assigned to the new counselor educator. This "mentor" was not in the counseling field, had been at the institution a number of years, and was not tenured. The "match" had been based on the mentor's request for a female protégé, her willingness to volunteer for the program, and her ability to "socialize" the new faculty member to the university's culture. The protégé was reluctant but felt pressured to participate so as not to hurt the assigned mentor's feelings and get off on the wrong foot at the institution. At the same time, the protégé was attempting to prepare new courses, to become familiar with the university, and to continue to progress toward tenure and promotion. After the first lunch meeting with the mentor, the protégé realized the assigned mentor had little to offer in terms of the actual tasks and political knowledge required to negotiate the organization. The mentor offered to meet for lunch and other social occasions on a number of times, and the female protégé politely declined. This resulted in the female mentor's feelings being hurt; however, it allowed the protégé time to get organized and to successfully complete her first semester at the new university.

Once the new counselor educator began to become familiar with the new university and its systems and procedures, she began to develop an informal mentoring relationship with a male, tenured counseling professor. He was familiar with the procedures necessary for gaining tenure and promotion, knew the social and political structure of the university community, had a similar background in counselor education, and was in a position of power to assist the new counselor educator in accessing the resources and opportunities necessary for success. For example, he assisted the female protégé in gaining access to committees to meet her service requirements, offered to copresent with her at state meetings, and introduced her to other counselor educators and faculty, which allowed her to begin to form her own network. From his position as department chair, he also was able to provide the female counselor educator with insight into the social and political history and climate of the organization. He used his experience and position to assist the female counselor educator in obtaining the necessary knowledge, skills, and resources to allow her to successfully obtain tenure and promotion. In addition, he provided support and encouragement. Following the female protégé's attainment of tenure and promotion, the male mentor was promoted to a higher administrative position in the university. He continued to mentor the female protégé by encouraging her to explore her aspirations to become an administrator in an institution that primarily consisted of male administrators. The female protégé benefited from this encouragement and support, and she became an entry-level administrator.

This example is particularly important because it illustrates several of the strengths and weaknesses of mentoring. First, there may be an implicit assumption that a female protégé may want or need a female mentor. A female mentor may not necessarily be in a position to provide the type of mentoring a female protégé may want or need.

Second, formal mentoring programs that assign mentor–protégé pairs must take into account the wants, needs, and characteristics of both the mentor and the protégé before the match is made. Third, even formal mentoring programs should provide opportunities for mentor and protégé to renegotiate the mentoring relationship, change mentor or protégé, or decline participation in the program. Fourth, it is essential that mentors have the necessary skills, knowledge, and experiences to assist the protégés who are assigned to them in formal programs. Fifth, the female protégé in this example was able to identify a male mentor and develop a mentoring relationship with him after she had been in the organization long enough to seek out an individual who could provide the knowledge, skills, and support she needed. Once she had identified this individual and he had expressed a willingness to act as a mentor, a mutually agreed-on mentoring relationship was able to develop that was of benefit to the protégé. Finally, in this example, the male mentor was in a position of power within the organization that he was willing to use to mentor the female protégé. In this way, he could continue to use his position and experience to provide access to opportunities for the female protégé that she may not have otherwise been able to access in a traditionally male environment.

Conclusion

Achieving a successful cross-gender mentoring relationship requires skills, interests, and efforts from the mentor, the protégé, and the organization. Both men and women must examine their assumptions, attitudes, and behaviors to ensure that they are not creating barriers to enhancing the cross-gender mentoring relationship. When both mentor and protégé have anticipated potential conflicts and barriers of a cross-gender mentoring relationship, a more effective and successful cross-gender mentoring relationship can be established. Organizations also must consider their role in either enhancing or suppressing cross-gender mentoring relationships.

References

Alleman, E., Cochran, J., Doverspire, J., & Newman, I. (1984). Enriching mentoring relationships. *The Personnel and Guidance Journal, 62,* 329–335.

Baugh, G., Lankau, M., & Scandura, T. A. (1996). An investigation of the effects of protégé gender on responses to mentoring. *Journal of Vocational Behavior, 49,* 309–323.

Beck, L. (1989). Mentorships: Benefits and effects on career development. *Gifted Child Quarterly, 33,* 22–28.

Bogat, G. A., & Redner, R. L. (1985). How mentoring affects the professional development of women in psychology. *Professional Psychology: Research and Practice, 16,* 851–859.

Brown-Wright, D. A., Dubick, R. A., & Newman, I. (1997). Graduate assistant expectation and faculty perception: Implications for mentoring and training. *Journal of College Student Development, 38,* 410–415.

Burke, R. J., McKeen, C. A., & McKenna, C. S. (1990). Sex differences and cross-sex effects on mentoring: Some preliminary data. *Psychological Reports, 67,* 1011–1023.

Clawson, J. G., & Kram, K. E. (1984). Managing cross gender mentoring. *Business Horizons, 27,* 22–32.

Collins, P. M., Kamya, H. A., & Tourse, R. W. (1997). Questions of racial diversity and mentorship: An empirical exploration. *Social Work, 42,* 145–152.

Erkut, S., & Mokros, J. R. (1984). Professors as models and mentors for college students. *American Educational Research Journal, 21,* 399–417.

Feist-Price, S. (1994). Cross gender mentoring relationships: Critical issues. *Journal of Rehabilitation, 60*(2), 13–17.

Gelberg, S., & Chojnacki, J. (1996). *Career and life planning with gay, lesbian, and bisexual persons.* Alexandria, VA: American Counseling Association.

Goldstein, E. (1979). Effect of same-sex and cross-sex models on the subsequent academic productivity of scholars. *American Psychologist, 34,* 407–410.

Graham, B. (1994). Mentoring and professional development in career services in higher education. *British Journal of Guidance and Counseling, 22,* 261–271.

Heimann, B., & Pittenger, K. K. S. (1996). The impact of formal mentorship on socialization and commitment of newcomers. *Journal of Managerial Issues, 8,* 108–117.

Hunt, D. M., & Michael, C. (1983). Mentorship: A career training and development tool. *Academy of Management Review, 8,* 475–485.

Kartje, J. V. (1996). O mentor! My mentor! *Peabody Journal of Education, 71,* 114–125.

Kram, K. E. (1985). *Mentoring at work.* Glenview, IL: Scott, Foresman.

McCormick, T. (1991). *An analysis of some pitfalls of traditional mentoring for minorities and women in higher education* (ERIC Document Reproduction Service No. ED 334 905). Greensboro, NC: Educational Resource Information Center.

Noe, R. A. (1988). An investigation of the determinants of successful assigned mentoring relationships. *Personnel Psychology, 41,* 457–479.

Ragins, R. B. (1989). Barriers to mentoring: The female manager's dilemma. *Human Relations, 42,* 1–22.

Ragins, R. B., & Cotton, J. L. (1993). Gender and willingness to mentor in organizations. *Journal of Management, 19,* 97–111.

Ragins, R. B., & McFarlin, D. B. (1990). Perceptions of mentor roles in cross gender mentoring relationships. *Journal of Vocational Behavior, 37,* 321–339.

Redmond, S. P. (1990). Mentoring and cultural diversity in academic settings. *American Behavioral Scientist, 34,* 188–200.

Scandura, T. A., & Ragins, B. R. (1993). The effects of sex and gender role orientation on mentorship in male-dominated occupations. *Journal of Vocational Behavior, 43,* 251–265.

Schwiebert, W. L., Deck, M. D., Bradshaw, M. L., Scott, P., & Harper, M. (1998). *Women as mentors.* Unpublished manuscript.

Scott, N. E. (1989). Differences in mentor relationships of non-White and White female professionals and organizational mobility: A review of the literature. *Psychology: A Journal of Human Behavior, 26,* 23–26.

Shapiro, E. C., Haseltine, F. P., & Rowe, M. P. (1978). Moving up: Role models, mentors, and the patron system. *Sloan Management Review, 19,* 51–58.

Turban, D. B., & Dougherty, T. W. (1994). Role of protégé personality in receipt of mentoring and career success. *Academy of Management Journal, 37,* 688–702.

Women as Mentors[1]

By Valerie L. Schwiebert

Historically, the first image of a mentor was that of a woman (see the reference to Homer's *The Odyssey* in chap. 1). However, in recent history, women have failed to realize the benefits that may be gained from participating in this powerful process. While men in the business world and other fields have reaped the benefits of mentoring relationships, women continue to be disadvantaged as a result of limited access to female mentors (Bizarri, 1995).

It is only recently that the importance of mentoring for women has begun to emerge. The purpose of this chapter is to provide a review of the literature related to women and mentoring. In addition, the roles and responsibilities assumed by female mentors and female mentees are discussed, and specific strategies are proposed for fostering effective mentoring relationships for and by women.

Barriers to Women Mentoring Women

The full potentials of women in society have not been attained in part because of the lack of women in highly visible public and pri-

---

[1]The material in this chapter first appeared in part as an article titled "Women as Mentors" in the *Journal of Humanistic Education and Development*, 1999, Vol. 37, pp. 241–253 by V. Schwiebert, M. Deck, M. Bradshaw, P. Scott, and M. Harper.

vate roles. This lack of visible female mentors and role models results in young girls being denied the opportunity to see and hear about ways in which women may attain these positions. Only in recent history has a woman been appointed as Attorney General of the United States, served as a Supreme Court Justice, or been a member of a Space Shuttle mission. This lack of visible female mentors results in young girls never even exploring the idea of trying to reach these positions, because they perceive that women cannot be president of the United States, head coaches of athletic teams, or chief executive officers in the corporate world.

In addition to a lack of role models, a distinct shortage of female role models in many fields has disadvantaged women in the pursuit of career choices and advancements (Bizzari, 1995). Researchers report that because of the lack of women in the upper echelons of their organizations, the pool of potential female mentors is proportionately much smaller than that of potential male mentors (Burke, McKeen, & McKenna, 1990; Cohen & Gutek, 1991; Dreher & Ash, 1990; Feist-Price, 1994; Noe, 1988; Reich, 1986; Sands, Parson, & Duane, 1991).

Although the number of successful women occupying positions of power continues to grow, historically, the research has shown that both male and female protégés are more likely to have male mentors (Feist-Price, 1994; Sands et al., 1991). Reasons cited for this were the dearth of female mentors available, males were traditionally older and had been employed longer with the same organization than their female counterparts, and male mentors were usually at a higher professional level (Burke et al., 1990; Sands et al., 1991).

Although a lack of available female mentors may explain some paucity of mentoring relationships for women, another factor may be that traditional models of mentoring have been developed on the basis of male models that stress masculine characteristics and interaction values. Many of these models have their roots in team sports and the military, neither of which reflects typical female experiences. Therefore, Ragins (1989) hypothesized that women may not have a referent for this type of relationship and may need to develop a different model of mentoring. Kalbfleisch (1994) proposed such a model that uses women's interpersonal and relational skills as strengths to be cultivated in the mentoring relationship.

In addition to the scarcity of female mentors available to female mentees, a review of the literature reveals a paucity of research specifically dedicated to female mentors with male protégés. Because of the lack of female mentors and the lack of women in advanced positions in organizations, cross-gender mentoring relationships are more prevalent among women than men (Noe, 1988). Therefore, many women have little choice but to have male mentors, if they are mentored at all. In addition, male mentees may not have access to female mentors and the unique benefits that may be obtained through establishing mentoring relationships with women. As the years have progressed, cross-gender mentoring has emerged as a subject of considerable controversy. This controversy is discussed further in the chapter on cross-gender mentoring.

Same-Gender Mentoring:
The Need for Women to Mentor Women

An alternative to the cross-gender mentoring relationship that may hold unique advantages for women is same-gender mentoring. Gilligan (1982), in her theory of women's psychological development, emphasized the importance of "making connections" in the lives of women. By this she meant that women tend to place a high degree of importance on communicating, feeling and caring about others, and having relationships. In a traditionally male world that is highly task-oriented, these female qualities may be perceived as weaknesses and undesirable traits rather than being perceived as unique strengths that women bring to the workplace. Therefore, many women may actively work to deny these traits and may cultivate traits that they perceive as more desirable, such as task-oriented behaviors. As a result, society ultimately loses because it fails to benefit from the strengths of being both task-oriented and relational, for each contributes equally to the development of the most successful approach.

The lack of visible and encouraging female role models can be especially detrimental for young girls during their early school years. The American Association of University Women Educational Foundation (AAUW), in its 1996 study of middle school girls, found that the involvement and nurturing of adult mentors, who were almost always cited as being women by the girls in the study, can be a critical factor to girls developing a sense of self during this time of growth and learning. The AAUW also cited the importance of offering girls choices when they are choosing mentors and including mentors of their own ethnic or cultural backgrounds who may be able to more fully understand struggles that may be unique to their situation. The lack of female mentors and role models is important not only for girls in their early years but also for women across the life span.

In 1992, Walker and Mehr published the results of an 8-year study of graduates of Hunter College, a college whose mission is to educate women. Walker and Mehr studied 1,250 women, ages 19 to 92, who graduated from the Hunter School for Girls. It is striking to note that 98% of those studied, whether they hated or loved their experience at Hunter, stated that the one missing aspect of their education was no counseling or guidance or that the guidance that they had received was unhelpful or perfunctory. While these women were working to complete an enriched educational program, they indicated that there was no one at Hunter whose specific job was to prepare them for obstacles and barriers they would face in the outside world. Their responses related particularly to the world of work, citing that they had no one to encourage them to pursue nontraditional roles or to inspire them to become leaders in their professions. Without this advice and nurturing, these students were left to rely on family and friends to assist them with career decisions and development, rather than the voices and experiences of other women who could function as mentors and role models.

Additionally, findings from Walker and Mehr's (1992) study showed that role models were lacking. Teachers were the most noted role models. However, students reported that teachers not only held their students to high academic achievements but also emphasized the traditional feminine pursuits and imparted a strong sense of social obligation and service to others. The overall effect of this type of role model was to deny one's intelligence and not to think of oneself as special. What teachers failed to do was to provide female students with models of how to serve society and others while still fulfilling their own visions and dreams.

Women in the Hunter study (Walker & Mehr, 1992) cited the following reasons for women not advancing in their careers. In their youth, being perfect little girls, lacking counseling and guidance, and having few nontraditional role models were cited. In adult life, having a lack of networking and mentoring in the workplace, experiencing isolation and discrimination on the job, and juggling family responsibilities and career with little assistance from spouse or employers were cited. Emotional components that were cited included an unwillingness to admit and be proud of the fact that they were smart, a fear of taking risks, and an inability to take responsibility for their choices.

Overall, Walker and Mehr's (1992) study emphasized that young girls and young women need successful women as role models and mentors. Teachers and counselors need to demonstrate and promote leadership skills, encourage young girls to explore and experiment with ideas and talents, and assist young girls and women in the development of visions and dreams. They need to challenge young girls and women to imagine themselves as leaders, heroes, and presidents and to encourage them to take risks and meet challenges. In adult life, Walker and Mehr's study emphasized the need for mentoring and networking in the workplace and strategies for women to overcome barriers of isolation, discrimination, and juggling family responsibilities and careers (Bizzari, 1995).

Female mentors and role models are in the perfect position to assist female mentees in these tasks. Female mentors may help the mentees gain access to a network of professionals by making the appropriate introductions and facilitating the development of professional relationships. The female mentors may encourage the mentees to attend professional meetings, become members of social and professional organizations, and provide the mentees with opportunities for networking.

In another study, Arnold (1993) reported the findings of a 10-year study of 46 female and 35 male high school valedictorians in the state of Illinois. She found that women demonstrated decreased intellectual self-esteem as early as their sophomore year of college and this decrease continued throughout their postdoctoral work. By 1991, some of the 46 women in the study were among the highest achievers in the study, but as a group, the women were achieving at lower levels than the men. Four other important findings came from this study. Women were found to perform equally to or at higher levels than men on all academic measures of achievement in the study. Women were equal to men on college entrance examination scores and college grade point averages; however, only women had lowered their estimates of their intelligence over their college years, whereas men had not. By their senior year in college, two thirds of the women in the study had planned to reduce or interrupt their careers for child rearing, whereas none of the men had planned interruptions in their careers. Finally, women's professional expectations as college seniors were found to be more vague than those of the men in the study. That is, men in the study listed specific occupations, levels, and professional settings, whereas women tended to report general career fields. Additionally, women were more likely than men to list multiple career possibilities.

Arnold's (1993) study indicates a developmental period when capable, achieving young women's perceptions of their abilities and career options seem to diminish in comparison with their actual performance abilities. At a time when women are exploring both their relational and career identities and roles, having female mentors and role models who have successfully integrated needs in both areas seems to be particularly important (Jeruchim & Shapiro, 1992).

One area in which same-gender mentoring may be extremely beneficial for women is in male-dominated careers (Bizzari, 1995). Atwater (1993) supported the importance of mentoring in areas typically not considered "female" interests. Females, especially minority females, must be encouraged and praised early and often when they express an interest or aptitude for these areas. Women who are successful in these fields also must make the commitment to share their knowledge and power and help guide young professionals who are entering these fields. Because only 9% of all engineers are women and only 7% of electrical engineers are women, this guidance is critical (Geppert, 1995).

Potential may also be lost when women do not know whom or how to ask for help in a male-dominated system. Men realize the importance of the mentoring relationship and use it to help other men negotiate the system. This may occur in overt as well as covert ways, such as talk in the locker room or conversations and connections made during a golf game or over drinks at a cocktail lounge. Women are usually excluded from participation in such events, particularly if they are seen as wives and mothers, in which case it may be deemed inappropriate for them to even wish to be included in such gatherings.

In addition, traditional male-to-male mentoring models rely on acceptance of the organizational hierarchy and are task-oriented. Women may desire a mentoring relationship that contains more opportunities for psychosocial and emotional support. According to Kram and Isabella (1985), this desire for a different type of mentoring relationship may lead women to look to their peers as a way to gain relational and emotional support at the expense of establishing mentoring relationships with higher ranking, influential mentors. Furthermore, women may believe that hard work, competence, and perseverance are more important determinants of success than forming ties with influential superiors (Nieva & Gutek, 1981). Conversely, men tend to recognize the importance of establishing these ties in order to climb the corporate ladder.

Even when a woman is in a visible position in a male-dominated career, it is usually a White woman and not a member of a minority group. Therefore, young girls who are looking for female mentors may be doubly disadvantaged because of the lack of women as role models and the lack of women who are members of their own ethnic or cultural group with whom they may identify. The importance of mentoring for women from diverse ethnic groups was highlighted in a study by Nora, Cabrera, Hagedorn, and Pascarella (1996), which examined a variety of factors that affected educational persistence in ethnic and gender groups at 4-year colleges. The researchers found that for women, mentoring experiences with faculty outside of the classroom setting was one of the most significant positive factors affecting educational persistence. A further discussion of the importance of a multicultural approach to mentoring is provided in a later chapter in this book.

The growth and development of women must be taken into consideration by female mentors. According to Gilligan (1982), women place importance on communication and feelings shared within relationships. As female mentors strive to allow for independent growth and development in mentees, they must create an atmosphere that allows time and respect for exploration of feelings that motivate individual decisions and choices. Time should be allowed to explore choices and decisions. Female mentors need to be active listeners as they guide their mentees to become strong in their professions and workplaces.

As women in the workplace, female mentors must consider their responsibilities in modeling competence and professionalism while encouraging appropriate assertive behaviors. Difficulties of women in professional settings include attempting to fit into culturally defined gender roles (Chao, Walz, & Gardner, 1992). Therefore, it is important that mentors provide role modeling that removes this perception. Female mentors can facilitate the development of leadership skills, foster self-confidence, and encourage assertiveness. An understanding of these components will help mentees to understand the system, its structure, players, politics, and their role within the whole.

Just as a characteristic for a mentoring relationship is to link the mentee with a network or support system, it is the responsibility of the female mentor to serve in promoting acceptance and entry into any profession as a woman. It is important for the female mentor to challenge the mentee to go beyond an expectation, to take a risk to reach her potential whether it is within a traditional or a novel role. The female mentor can help establish networks and support systems that allow the female mentee to meet this challenge. The responsibility to share resources as female mentors allows women to address competition versus collaboration and cooperation.

It is interesting to note that there are numerous programs aimed at helping women remedy perceived "deficiencies" in their way of relating in a male-dominated world. Programs such as "Assertiveness Training for Women," "Corporate Communications for Women," and "Keys to Success for Women in Business" all suggest an implied deficiency that women must remedy by attending these workshops designed to make them more competitive in a male-dominated world. This "deficiencies" model of assisting women in career advancement perpetuates the devaluation of female attributes (e.g., relational skills, empathy, and nurturance) and continues to reinforce the idea that the more male attributes (e.g., power and task orientation) are more desirable and valuable. Thus, the entire world of work remains based on the male model of "getting ahead," and society does not benefit from the inclusion and valuing of more female attributes.

These responsibilities help the mentee ultimately make the transition from mentee to colleague. This is the goal in any mentoring relationship. The mentoring relationship should be considered a dynamic interaction that transforms as the mentee and the mentor grow within it. Just as the mentor has responsibilities that allow for the reaching of the final outcome, so does the mentee. The following section defines the responsibilities of the female mentee.

Responsibilities and Characteristics of Mentees

Just as some of the responsibilities discussed in relation to mentor roles can be generalized to a variety of mentoring relationships, responsibilities of the mentee also can be generalized. However, women as mentees introduce differences within the mentoring relationship. Characteristics of mentee personalities (Turban & Dougherty, 1994), as well as mentee gender (Baugh, Lankau, & Scandura, 1996), influence mentoring outcomes.

The main component of mentee responsibilities is the understanding that the mentee is a partner in the mentoring process (Daresh & Playko, 1995). The mentee role is not a passive role but rather an active one. As such, the mentee must recognize that she may not simply receive information and advice but must participate to facilitate an effective, dynamic relationship. Female mentees may capitalize on their relational strengths to build the mentoring relationship. However, they also may be called on to use assertive skills and to balance their own need for psychosocial and emotional support with the mentor's ability to provide such support.

It may be necessary for the mentee to search out several different mentoring relationships in order to meet all of her needs. For example, she may establish one mentoring relationship with a powerful woman who has achieved success in her profession. This woman may have focused on professional achievement and chosen not to add the roles of wife and mother. A mentee who may wish to achieve professionally and be a wife and a mother may wish to seek additional role models who have become successful professionals while also being wives and mothers. In addition, the mentee may wish to establish mentoring relationships with other professionals who provide relational and emotional support that may be missing in her other relationships. Finally, she also may wish to establish cross-gender mentoring relationships in order to gain this perspective as well.

Strategies for Fostering Female Mentoring Relationships

Mentors can use several different strategies for fostering effective mentoring relationships. One of the first steps in developing an effective mentoring program includes an examination of the culture of the organization to identify facilitating and inhibiting factors for mentoring women. Another step includes recognizing the importance of mentoring by incorporating mentoring activities into performance evaluation criteria and into formal programs sanctioned by the organization. This provides an internal reward and recognition system for mentors and mentees. In addition, formal programs sanctioned by the organization may reduce misperceptions of mentoring relationships, particularly cross-gender mentoring relationships.

Creating formal and informal opportunities for mentors and mentees to interact is another step in developing mentoring relationships. These opportunities should include female mentoring relationships, which may be cultivated across developmental levels and at all levels within the organization. These opportunities allow female mentees access to multiple mentors, which may allow them to benefit most fully from the mentoring process.

Training programs may be established that teach interested women how to become effective mentors, particularly mentors to other women. Topics that may be included are how to establish a mentoring relationship, the importance of mentoring, gender differences in mentoring, the appropriate boundaries of a mentoring relationship, and the ultimate termination of the mentoring relationship as the mentee makes the transition to colleague. Support systems may be established to allow mentors to share effective strategies and concerns and to develop their mentoring skills.

Finally, the mentoring relationship may be more effective if mentors and mentees discuss and define their relationship by considering questions such as: What is a good mentor? What is a good role model? What kind of feedback do mentors and mentees need? What do mentees and mentors owe each other?

Perhaps professional counseling organizations such as Chi Sigma Iota International, whose mission is to help prepare future leaders in the profession, could begin to include training on how to be a mentor and a mentee in their leadership training. In addition, counselor education programs could include information on mentoring in their introductory classes for beginning counseling students. This information could help counseling students realize the power of the mentoring process, how to locate mentors, what to expect from the relationship, and what to do if problems arise. Some counseling programs have already initiated mentoring programs in which 2nd-year students offer to be paired with incoming counseling students for the purpose of mentoring. These are only a few ways that counselors, counselor educators, and counseling students may heighten their awareness of the mentoring process.

Conclusion

In conclusion, there exists a great need for female mentors. Although cross-gender mentoring relationships are more prevalent than same-gender mentoring relationships, women may gain greater benefits from participating in a same-gender mentoring relationship. Mentoring relationships in which women are mentored by other women provide the mentees with both psychosocial and career development benefits. Mentoring relationships in which women are mentored by men are more often based on career development, lack the relational component important to many women, and fail to provide role models with whom women can identify. However, because both types of mentoring have unique benefits, perhaps the most beneficial mentoring includes mentors from both genders or multiple mentors.

Men have realized the benefits of the mentoring process and continue to use this process to assist other men in becoming professionals in many fields. Women have only recently become aware of the importance of the mentoring process, particularly the process of women mentoring other women. As women continue to progress in the attainment of advanced positions, more potential female role models and mentors become available. It is incumbent on these women to realize the power they possess as role models and mentors and to actively cultivate mentoring relationships with other women. In this way, the daughters of Athena, centuries later, may realize their relational as well as their career potentials and find a mentor, a role model, a friend, and a colleague to advise and trust (Lawrence, 1985).

References

American Association of University Women Educational Foundation. (1996). *Girls in the middle: Working to succeed in school.* Washington, DC: Author.

Arnold, K. (1993). Academically talented women in the 1980's: The Illinois Valedictorian Project. In K. Hulbert & D. Schuster (Eds.), *Women's lives through time: Educated American women of the twentieth century* (pp. 393–416). San Francisco: Jossey-Bass.

Atwater, M. M. (1993). Multicultural science education. *The Science Teacher, 60,* 33–38.

Baugh, G., Lankau, M., & Scandura, T. A. (1996). An investigation of the effects of protégé gender on responses to mentoring. *Journal of Vocational Behavior, 49,* 309–323.

Bizzari, J. (1995, Spring). Women: Role models, mentors, and careers. *Educational Horizons,* 145–152.

Burke, R., McKeen, C., & McKenna, C. (1990). Sex differences and cross sex effects on mentoring: Some preliminary data. *Psychological Reports, 67,* 1111–1123.

Chao, G. T., Walz, P. M., & Gardner, P. D. (1992). Formal and informal mentorships: A comparison on mentoring functions and contrasts with non-mentored counterparts. *Personnel Psychology, 45,* 619–636.

Cohen, A., & Gutek, B. (1991). Sex differences in the career experiences of members of two APA divisions. *American Psychologist, 46,* 1292–1298.

Daresh, J. C., & Playko, M. A. (1995, April). *Mentoring in educational leadership development: What are the responsibilities of the protégés?* Paper presented at the meeting of the American Education Research Association, San Francisco.

Dreher, G., & Ash, R. A. (1990). A comparative study of mentoring among men and women in managerial, professional, and technical positions. *Journal of Applied Psychology, 75,* 539–546.

Feist-Price, S. (1994). Cross gender mentoring relationships: Critical issues. *Journal of Rehabilitation, 60*(2), 13–17.

Geppert, L. (1995). The uphill struggle: No rose garden for women in engineering. *IEEE Spectrum, 32*(5), 40–51.

Gilligan, C. (1982). *In a different voice: Psychological theory and women's development.* Cambridge, MA: Harvard University Press.

Jeruchim, J., & Shapiro, P. (1992). *Women, mentors, and success.* New York: Fawcett Columbine.

Kalbfleisch, P. J. (1994, April). *The mentoring relationships of women and men.* Paper presented at the annual meeting of the Western States Communication Association, San Jose, CA.

Kram, K. E., & Isabella, L. A. (1985). Mentoring alternatives: The role of peer relationships in career development. *Academy of Management Journal, 28,* 110–132.

Lawrence, K. (1985, October). *My key to the men's room. Mentor and protégé relationships in business and professional organizations: An overview.* Paper presented at the annual meeting of the Central States Speech Association, Indianapolis, IN.

Nieva, V., & Gutek, B. (1981). Sex effects on evaluation. *Academy of Management Review, 5,* 267.

Noe, R. A. (1988). An investigation of the determinants of successful assigned mentoring relationships. *Personnel Psychology, 41,* 457–479.

Nora, A., Cabrera, A., Hagedorn, L. S., & Pascarella, E. (1996). Differential impacts of academic and social experiences on college-related behavioral outcomes across different ethnic and gender groups at four-year institutions. *Research in Higher Education, 37,* 427–451.

Ragins, B. (1989). Barriers to mentoring: The female manager's dilemma. *Human Relations, 42,* 1–22.

Reich, M. H. (1986). The mentor connection. *Personnel, 63,* 50–56.

Sands, R. G., Parson, L. A., & Duane, J. (1991). Faculty mentoring faculty in a public university. *Journal of Higher Education, 62,* 174–193.

Turban, D., & Dougherty, D. (1994) Role of the protégé personality in receipt of mentoring and career success. *Academy of Management Journal, 37,* 688–702.

Walker, B., & Mehr, M. (1992). *The courage to achieve: Why America's brightest women struggle to fulfill their promise.* New York: Simon & Schuster.

CHAPTER

Multicultural Aspects of the Mentoring Process

By June Williams and Valerie L. Schwiebert

*A*lthough the 1990s have been a decade in which multiculturalism has been at the forefront of the counseling literature (Lee, 1997; Pedersen, 1994; Sue & Sue, 1990), discussions of mentoring as a multicultural process among counselors have yet to occur. In fact, multicultural implications for the mentoring process have been given only cursory attention in the literature. Because this book is a pioneering effort to stimulate dialogue and action among counselors regarding mentoring processes and issues in counseling, this chapter is intended to present an overview of multicultural issues that may impact the mentoring process. Research on mentoring from other areas such as business and education are used to supplement the paucity of specific literature related to multicultural issues and mentoring in the counselor education literature.

This chapter provides a definition of multiculturalism and attempts to highlight multicultural issues that may impact the mentoring process. Additionally, topics discussed include problems in applying traditional concepts of mentoring to diverse populations, the lack of available mentors for ethnic minority groups, lack of access to the mentoring process, benefits and challenges of cross-cultural mentoring, and the need for mentors and role models who are representative of a diverse population. Finally, implications for counselors and suggestions for developing diversified mentoring relationships are presented.

Multiculturalism Defined

Several definitions of multiculturalism have been proposed in the literature, ranging in scope from broad, inclusive definitions to narrow, specific definitions. For the purposes of this chapter, we borrowed from Lee's (1997) definition of culture as ethnicity because most of the discussions of multicultural mentoring primarily have focused on ethnic minority groups. Studies reported in the literature have concentrated mostly on multicultural implications of mentoring for Black men, although a few have focused on Black women and Latinos. This limitation must be considered when one is attempting to generalize the findings of these studies to other populations.

Although the benefits of mentoring for both mentors and mentees have been widely acknowledged and discussed earlier in this book, the primary beneficiaries of the mentoring process have been a limited population, namely European American males (Atkinson, Casas, & Neville, 1994). Traditional mentoring has been the path to success for White men and, for the most part, has excluded ethnic minority groups (McCormick, 1997). The belief that mentoring relationships are readily available for all who seek them is one of the misconceptions identified by Kram (1985). European American women and ethnic minority groups typically have been underrepresented in the mentoring process (Blackwell, 1989).

Applying Traditional Mentoring Models to Diverse Populations

Although existing literature regarding mentoring describes particular programs or models that address an organization's or a group's specific needs, no models, as yet, have been identified or tested in a variety of settings to generalize to multicultural mentoring (Gonzalez-Rodriguez, 1995). Additionally, Ragins (1997a, 1997b) argued that emerging mentoring theories do not adequately address the influence of diversity on these relationships. Gonzalez-Rodriguez (1995) stated that "the traditional model of mentoring imposes a monocultural perspective and an assimilationist goal" (p. 73). Traditionally, mentoring has been monocultural because it has been the purview of European American men, limiting the involvement of women and minority groups. By "assimilationist," Gonzalez-Rodriguez is referring to the intention of the dominant Western culture to maintain the status quo, thereby requiring minority groups to adopt the values of the majority system.

The monocultural perspective of traditional mentoring also has been criticized by McCormick (1997), who noted that the model of White male mentoring must be transformed so that it can be applicable to minorities and women. Gonzalez-Rodriguez (1995) argued that Minnuch's (1990) theory of "alterity" is related to the perpetuation of a monocultural concept of mentoring. Minnuch defined alterity as one person viewing another person as strange, different, or inferior, thus distant from himself or herself. When one holds this belief, one believes that particular groups (i.e., dominant groups) are the ones that should set the standards for all people. This prevents meaningful interactions between members of various cultural groups.

McCormick (1997) also criticized the assimilationist goal of traditional mentoring, noting that such an approach socializes mentees into the "rules of the game" that they must learn before becoming a part of the inner circle, which is discriminatory toward women and minorities. In a study of minority faculty members, Brinson and Kottler (1993) observed that beginning minority faculty often feel very much alone and that these feelings of isolation are increased if they believe that they must surrender aspects of their cultural identity in an attempt to fit into the existing environment. Historically, assimilation has been the only available option for members of ethnic minority groups (Garcia, 1995); however, multiculturalism represents a resistance to the cultural amalgamation of the American melting pot, which limits the number of pathways leading to successful integration.

Inherent in the traditional concept of mentoring is the power that the older, wiser mentor holds in the relationship (Gonzalez-Rodriguez, 1995). Mentoring is historically a hierarchical and patriarchal rather than a communal or collaborative relationship (Bova, 1995; Gonzalez-Rodriguez, 1995). The assumption is that the protégé will follow in the footsteps of the mentor and maintain the status quo (Gonzalez-Rodriguez, 1995). McCormick (1997) observed that European American men have used mentoring as a tool to remain in positions of power. Similarly, traditional mentoring models place a great deal of emphasis on individual achievement and competition, which can be a source of conflict for individuals whose cultures value cooperation and group cohesiveness (Bova, 1995). By promoting competition and focusing on personal ambition, traditional mentoring promotes elitism and exclusion (McCormick, 1997).

Multiculturally Inclusive Mentoring

The existing literature that addresses issues of diversity in mentoring is critical of the traditional structures and suggests that alternative models be considered to address the issue of diversity. Recent theories of mentoring have failed to address the issue of diversity (Ragins, 1997a, 1997b). Gonzalez-Rodriguez (1995) noted that the vagueness regarding what constitutes mentoring complicates the notion of multicultural mentoring as well as efforts to address issues of diversity through mentoring.

A major consideration in culturally inclusive mentoring is to provide groups that traditionally have been excluded from mentoring relationships with an opportunity to participate. Welch (1997) stated that to be effective, a comprehensive mentoring model with underrepresented groups must foster the kind of equity that encourages discourse, critical dialogue, and an understanding of the role of power. Inherent in such an inclusive model is an emphasis on dialogue between mentors and their protégés regarding their unique experiences, personalities, interests, and backgrounds. According to Gonzalez-Rodriguez (1995), multicultural mentoring creates spaces for differences and celebrates democracy by facilitating inclusion and participation. It allows learning to take place while ensuring that no one's voice is silenced.

This learning is at the heart of multicultural mentoring. Gonzalez-Rodriguez (1995) described learning as an active process that is deeply contextualized and developmental. Thus, there is no one right way to mentor; it is dependent on a multitude of factors, one of which is cultural background.

Diversified mentoring is both ambitious and demanding; it requires knowledge, skills, openness, fairness, discipline, commitment, and courage (Gonzalez-Rodriguez, 1995). Multiculturally inclusive mentoring requires a commitment from the organization or institution, because the institution's values, commitment, and structures will be questioned. The process of mentoring in such an environment encourages dialogue, feedback, and honesty on the part of both the mentor and the protégé.

To encourage more participation in mentoring among ethnic minority groups and to improve the quality of mentoring, potential mentors must seriously consider the developmental nature of the process itself. When mentor and protégé view each other as individuals in the process of development rather than as superiors or subordinates, the power and hierarchy are diminished and may be replaced by collaboration and openness. Such a model will hopefully facilitate and encourage participation among typically underrepresented populations, particularly those individuals who place a high value on collaboration versus a more hierarchical structure.

Cross-Cultural Versus Monocultural Mentoring

Researchers are divided in their support for the importance of matching mentors and mentees according to cultural background (Jacobi, 1991). Pairing mentors by ethnicity is problematic for minority individuals because of the reality that, by nature, minority groups are underrepresented and, therefore, have fewer potential mentors and protégés from whom to choose (Haring, 1996). In studies of Black individuals, race was the best predictor of pairings in mentorships, with mentors typically selecting mentees who were similar to themselves (Blackwell, 1989; Kalbfleisch & Davies, 1991). Carter (1982) observed that mentoring is most effective when the individuals involved share similar values, attitudes, goals, and worldviews. Thus, the most likely mentor–protégé partnerships are between individuals from similar backgrounds rather than different backgrounds. The lack of available culturally similar role models may be accentuated by the cultural bias to mentor those from similar backgrounds (Blackwell, 1989) and taboos against cross-cultural mentoring (Thomas, 1989).

An important issue in multicultural mentoring is that of trust. Especially in relationships in which the individuals differ in cultural backgrounds, numerous sociocultural factors exist that present challenges (Pedersen, 1994). Members of ethnic minority groups often enter into relationships with European Americans experiencing feelings of mistrust because of the historical relationships between the cultures. These feelings present a barrier that must be overcome prior to achieving the intimacy and trust necessary for a productive and effective mentoring relationship (Brinson & Kottler, 1993). For the protégé and the mentor to develop trust, each individual must be sensitive to the other's uniqueness and how his or her cultural background and previous experiences have contributed to his or her development (Brinson & Kottler, 1993).

When individuals from diverse backgrounds are paired together, misunderstandings are very common (Brinson & Kottler, 1993). These misunderstandings often result in perceived slights, which likely are the result of ignorance or insensitivity rather than malevolence (Brinson & Kottler, 1993). In Bova's (1995) study of Hispanic women in higher education, all of the women highly valued the importance of developing quality relationships with both their students and colleagues. All of these women placed a high value on listening, a value not evident in many of their workplaces. Bova also discovered that one of the major causes of stress and low recognition was cultural communication conflict. Effective personal communication, listening, and cooperation are important aspects of mentoring relationships, particularly for ethnic minority individuals (Redmond, 1990).

Another potential problem inherent in cross-cultural pairings is stereotyping (Bova, 1995; Brinson & Kottler, 1993). According to Sue and Sue (1990), stereotypes occur when characteristics of certain groups are generalized to all members regardless of individual differences. Ragins (1997b) noted that minority individuals often are perceived as less competent because of stereotypes. Because of these negative perceptions, their power within an organization and, thus, their status are unjustly underrated.

Despite the problems previously identified in cross-cultural mentoring relationships, Brinson and Kottler (1993) identified several benefits of such relationships for both partners. The development of successful multicultural mentoring relationships provides both individuals and organizations with positive models of collaboration and respect that may exist between members of differing cultural and ethnic backgrounds. Mentors and protégés who are from different ethnic backgrounds must teach and learn from each other, thus demonstrating unity and acceptance of values. A second benefit is that both members of the relationship are provided with an opportunity to expand their awareness and understanding of individuals from different backgrounds. Thus, Brinson and Kottler argued that cross-cultural mentoring assists in broadening the perspectives of scholars, theoreticians, and researchers by facilitating the generalization of ideas between and among diverse populations.

For cross-cultural mentoring relationships to be effective, however, certain qualities must be present in both mentors and protégés (Brinson & Kottler, 1993). First, mentors must be genuinely concerned about the personal welfare of protégés regardless of their cultural or ethnic background. Second, mentors must possess the expertise, position, and inclination to be helpful in the protégés' professional development. Third, mentors need to be culturally sensitive and willing to devote time to learn about the protégés' ethnic heritage. Finally, mentors must appreciate the protégés' individuality and how they may differ from others from the same culture.

Protégés must also be willing to share their own cultural and ethnic experiences with the mentors so that the mentors can understand the protégés' perspectives and needs. Protégés must also be willing to learn about the mentors' experiences and cultural background. Finally, protégés must be willing to appreciate the mentors as individuals and not merely as representatives of the groups they represent. This may mean overcoming preconceived prejudices regarding individuals from the mentors' background.

Formal Versus Informal Mentoring

A great deal of the discussion in the mentoring literature centers on formal, structured mentoring programs as opposed to natural, spontaneous mentoring relationships. In an effort to recruit and retain employees and students, particularly underrepresented populations, many organizations have initiated formal, structured mentoring programs that connect entry-level employees or students with more experienced individuals. Often, an effort is made to pair individuals with someone of the same cultural background; however, as mentioned in the previous section, this is often difficult because of the lack of available mentors. Nevertheless, formal mentoring programs may help to increase the possibility of advancement for ethnic groups (Redmond, 1990).

A great deal of the recent research, however, has been critical of formal mentoring programs. Haring (1996) noted that the majority of structured programs follow the grooming model and are not responsive to the needs of minorities. Other criticisms are that the relationships in assigned pairings are more superficial than the relationships in spontaneous pairings (Kram, 1985) and that chemistry and commitment between individuals cannot be legislated (Fagerson-Eland, Marks, & Amendda, 1997).

In contrast to formal mentoring programs, which typically assign specific mentees to specific mentors, informal mentoring relationships develop naturally as a result of personal interests and relationships (Gonzalez-Rodriguez, 1995). Many of the critics of formal mentoring programs are more supportive of the development of informal mentoring relationships. Informal relationships tend to be long-term, multifaceted, and potentially profound in impact. These relationships are ideal for culturally diverse populations because individuals may enter into relationships with individuals with whom they feel comfortable and share enough in common to sustain the relationship. These natural pairings may or may not be between individuals from similar ethnic backgrounds.

Another form of mentoring that actually may be either structured or unstructured (i.e., formal or informal) is networking. Networking provides opportunities for individuals to receive mentoring from multiple individuals rather than relying on one individual to fulfill all of the mentoring roles and responsibilities. In a study of Hispanic women in higher education, Bova (1995) observed that most of the women had multiple mentors, different individuals who provided the various functions of the traditional mentor's role. Bova described these relationships by using the analogy of a hub with several spokes, where the protégé is the center or hub controlling the spokes (multiple mentors) rather than the more hierarchical ladder type of relationship. Cox (1993) argued that informal contacts and networks are crucial for professional advancement because they provide individuals with information regarding the institution's values and systems.

In a study of graduate students from underrepresented populations from a variety of settings, students and their mentors preferred network mentoring models because of the increased availability of mentors as well as encouragement of reciprocity (Haring, 1996). Network models of mentoring possess egalitarian characteristics (Welch, 1997). Additional benefits of network mentoring relationships are the flexibility and individuality provided as mentors and protégés move through various stages (Welch, 1997). This type of mentoring provides members of underrepresented groups with more opportunities to engage in mentoring relationships (Schockett & Haring-Hidore, 1985).

Cox (1993) cautioned ethnic minority protégés against relying exclusively on culturally based informal networks as a springboard for promotion or advancement. Because in most organizations the power remains in the hands of majority group members, minority protégés need the support and encouragement of the majority group in order to advance. In a study of Black students, Blackwell

(1989) found that network mentoring can be effective and can complement formal mentoring programs.

Formal and informal mentoring, therefore, are not mutually exclusive. Encouraging the development of informal relationships, possibly even multiple mentors, may enhance formal mentoring programs and provide increased opportunities for members of traditionally underrepresented populations to benefit from access to both members of the majority group and members of their own cultural group (Terrell & Hassell, 1994).

Multicultural Issues and Mentoring in Counseling

According to the minority identity model developed by Sue (1981), members of minority cultures may progress through five psychosocial stages of cultural identity development. These stages include conformity, dissonance, resistance and immersion, introspection, and synergetic articulation and awareness. In the conformity stage, the individual is self-deprecating and prefers to be identified with the dominant culture values. In the dissonance stage, the individual develops conflicts between dominant culture and his or her own culture that lead to a state of cultural confusion. In the resistance and immersion stage, the individual is more self-deprecating and actively rejects the dominant society. In the introspection stage, the individual evaluates his or her own attitude toward self and the dominant society. Finally, in the synergetic articulation and awareness stage, the individual accepts his or her own cultural identity and develops a selective appreciation of the dominant culture.

The stages of minority identity development have implications for mentoring relationships. Individuals in different stages of identity development may have differing needs and issues to be recognized and dealt with in the mentoring relationship. This may occur whether there is a cross-cultural mentoring relationship or a same-cultural minority mentoring relationship. That is, individuals from underrepresented groups may be at differing stages of minority identity development and therefore have differing needs and concerns. These differences may either help or hurt the mentoring relationship. For example, if a Black female mentor is in the synergetic articulation and awareness stage and a Black female protégé is in the resistance and immersion stage, conflicts may arise regarding the mentor's selective appreciation of the dominant culture and the protégé's active rejection of the dominant culture. This conflict may hinder the mentoring relationship. Individuals at the same stage of minority identity development may find common issues with which they are currently struggling. This may be positive in facilitating a connection between the individuals but negative in that neither individual may have the experience to help the other grow.

Recognition and understanding of the stages of minority identity development benefits both dominant-culture mentors and protégés and minority mentors and protégés involved in multicultural mentoring relationships. If the individuals involved recognize one another's current stage of development and respect the implications of the current stage of development for the individual's worldview, then effective mentoring can occur.

Culturally effective mentors may need to possess the same types of skills necessary for culturally effective counselors. These include an ability to recognize the mentor's own values and assumptions related to human behavior, mentor awareness of the mentoring skills that cut across groups of individuals, and mentor awareness of the sociopolitical forces that influence the development of culturally different individuals. Mentors also may need both the ability to share the worldview of their protégés without negating its legitimacy and the ability to refrain from imposing their own values on others (Sue, 1978).

Counselors possess training in multicultural issues and should be familiar with the competencies necessary for effective counseling with culturally different individuals. It is imperative that counselors use this knowledge and training in designing mentoring programs that meet the needs of those who may be either culturally different mentors or protégés. Counselors may design training for potential mentors working in multicultural mentoring relationships. In addition, they may use this knowledge when developing mentoring pairs to optimize the chances of a successful mentoring relationship.

The following case example, based on an actual cross-cultural mentoring relationship, may serve to highlight some of the issues that may arise in such mentoring relationships. A junior, White, female administrator is hired by a Black male administrator. The two administrators are employed in a predominately White male institution located in the southern United States. The woman was born and raised in the Northeast. The man previously lived and worked extensively in the South. The mentor and the protégé had known each other as administrator and faculty member before the protégé took the entry-level administrative position. They had begun to develop a working relationship prior to her move to the new position, and the protégé had developed a deep respect for the senior administrator on the basis of his leadership style. The protégé particularly admired the administrator's ability to inspire trust, take a position and act on it, follow through on his commitments, and laugh in the face of adversity. These factors were very influential in her decision to accept the beginning administrative position. Therefore, she entered into the new position with the intention of establishing a protégé–mentor relationship with the Black senior administrator. Her hope was that she could learn to integrate the leadership characteristics he displayed into her own leadership style.

After the protégé had been in the position for some time, she began to feel pressure from colleagues and other administrators to fall into one of two stereotypical categories, "female executive" or "White male executive." The female stereotype carried the implicit traits of being less powerful, more relational (seen as a negative trait), and more subservient. The male stereotype carried the implicit traits of establishing dominance and hierarchy, minimizing relational behaviors, and assuming the traditional role of White male executive.

The female protégé became very frustrated and disillusioned when faced with these "choices." She approached her mentor and related these frustrations. In the course of the conversation, she told the mentor of her reluctance to choose either position and how she felt pressured to do so. Her frustration culminated in a statement to her mentor that sounded something like, "You just don't understand what it is like to be a female in an organization dominated by White men." Her mentor, in his typical style, began to smile and then laugh. The female protégé, realizing the humor in her own statement, also began to laugh. The two then had a long conversation regarding the pressures of being a member of an underrepresented group. This conversation culminated in the mentor helping the protégé to see that she did not have to choose to conform to either style but could choose to develop her own style. The mentor's support, empathy, understanding, and advice helped the protégé leave the meeting feeling validated and with a vision of how she could indeed shape her own style of leadership.

This example highlights several issues associated with multicultural mentoring relationships. It is also an interesting example because it involves cross-gender as well as multicultural mentoring.

The mentor in this example had life experiences and professional experiences that made him sensitive to the issues faced by the female protégé. His position as a Black man in a traditional organization allowed him to empathize with the protégé in a way that created rapport and trust. In addition, he had developed his own style of leadership partially due to the fact that he was not a member of the traditional system and therefore was able to provide additional options to the protégé that he knew had worked in practice. He was able to draw on his experiences to provide support, validation, and appropriate guidance for the protégé. Although he was not a woman, he had lived firsthand the experiences of being a member of an underrepresented group in an administrative position. This allowed the mentor and the protégé to share a common ground. The mentor had attained the synergetic articulation and awareness stage of racial identity development. He was able to use that worldview to help the protégé develop selective appreciation of the dominant leadership styles but also to allow for a different leadership style based on his cultural identity and worldview. The protégé benefited not only from the similar experiences her mentor brought to the relationship but also from sharing and discussing the different challenges that each of them faced. In this instance, the multicultural nature of the mentoring relationship provided benefits and alternatives for the protégé that a typical mentoring relationship might not have provided if the mentor had been another woman or a White man.

Conclusion

The issue of cultural diversity in mentoring relationships is a phenomenon that has only recently begun to be explored. The fields of business and education have begun to explore these issues and have identified some problems in traditional mentoring approaches as well as suggested alternative approaches that are more sensitive to cultural differences. The traditional mentoring models that are hierarchical, are focused primarily on career advancement, and promote cultural assimilation are not effective for individuals from ethnic minority backgrounds. Approaches that espouse cooperation rather than competition, egalitarianism rather than hierarchical relationships, and acceptance of cultural differences rather than assimilation are likely to be the most effective for culturally diverse groups. In addition, although formal mentoring programs may be effective and may ensure that no one is excluded, they are most productive when they are used simultaneously with more informal networking types of relationships.

References

Atkinson, D. R., Casas, A., & Neville, H. (1994). Ethnic minority psychologists: Whom they mentor and benefits they derive from the process. *Journal of Multicultural Counseling and Development, 22,* 37–48.

Blackwell, J. E. (1989). Mentoring: An action strategy for increasing minority faculty. *Academe, 75,* 8–14.

Bova, B. M. (1995). Mentoring revisited: The Hispanic woman's perspective. *Journal of Adult Education, 23,* 8–19.

Brinson, J., & Kottler, J. (1993). Cross-cultural mentoring in counselor education: A strategy for retaining minority faculty. *Counselor Education and Supervision, 32,* 241–253.

Carter, H. (1982, March). *Making it in academia: Gurus can get you there?* Paper presented at the annual meeting of the American Educational Research Association, New York.

Cox, T. (1993). *Cultural diversity in organizations: Theory, research, and practice.* San Francisco: Benett Koehler.

Fagerson-Eland, A., Marks, M. A., & Amendda, K. L. (1997). Perceptions of mentoring relationships. *Journal of Vocational Behavior, 51,* 29–42.

Garcia, J. A. (1995). A multicultural America: Living in a sea of diversity. In D. A. Harris (Ed.), *Multiculturalism from the margins: Non-dominant voices of difference and diversity* (pp. 29–38). Westport, CT: Bergin & Garvey.

Gonzalez-Rodriguez, X. E. (1995). Mentoring to diversity: A multicultural approach. *New Directions for Adult and Continuing Education, 66,* 69–77.

Haring, M. J. (1996). Networking mentoring as a preferred model for guiding programs for underrepresented students. In H. T. Frierson (Ed.), *Diversity in higher education: Mentoring and diversity in higher education* (Vol. 1, pp. 63–76). Greenwich, CT: JAI Press.

Jacobi, M. (1991). Mentoring and undergraduate academic success: A literature review. *Review of Educational Research, 61,* 505–532.

Kalbfleisch, P. J., & Davies, A. B. (1991). Minorities and mentoring: Managing the multicultural institution. *Communication Education, 40,* 266–271.

Kram, K. (1985). *Mentoring at work.* Boston: Scott, Foresman.

Lee, C. (1997). *Multicultural issues in counseling: New approaches to diversity* (2nd ed.). Alexandria, VA: American Counseling Association.

McCormick, T. (1997). An analysis of five pitfalls of traditional mentoring for people on the margins in higher education. In H. T. Frierson (Ed.), *Diversity in higher education: Mentoring and diversity in higher education* (Vol. 1, pp. 187–202). Greenwich, CT: JAI Press.

Minnuch, E. (1990). *Transforming knowledge.* Philadelphia: Temple University Press.

Pedersen. P. (1994). *Handbook for developing multicultural awareness* (2nd ed.). Alexandria, VA: American Association for Counseling and Development.

Ragins, B. R. (1997a). Antecedents of diversified mentoring relationships. *Journal of Vocational Behavior, 51,* 90–109.

Ragins, B. R. (1997b). Diversified mentoring relationships in organizations: A power approach. *Academy of Management Review, 22,* 482–492.

Redmond, S. P. (1990). Mentoring and cultural diversity in academic settings. *American Behavioral Scientist, 34,* 188–200.

Schockett, M., & Haring-Hidore, M. (1985). Factor analytic support for psychosocial and vocational mentoring functions. *Psychological Reports, 57,* 627–632.

Sue, D. W. (1978). Counseling across cultures. *Personnel and Guidance Journal, 56,* 451.

Sue, D. W. (1981). *Counseling the culturally different.* New York: Wiley.

Sue, D. W., & Sue, D. (1990). *Counseling the culturally different: Theory and practice* (2nd ed.). New York: Wiley.

Terrell, M. C., & Hassell, R. K. (1994). Mentoring undergraduate minority students: An overview, survey, and model program. *New Directions for Teaching and Learning, 57,* 33–43.

Thomas, D. A. (1989). Mentoring and irrationality: The role of racial taboos. *Human Resource Management, 28,* 279–290.

Welch, O. (1997). An examination of effective mentoring models in academe. In H. T. Frierson (Ed.), *Diversity in higher education: Mentoring and diversity in higher education* (Vol. 1, pp. 41–62). Greenwich, CT: JAI Press.

Programs and Models of Mentoring

By Valerie L. Schwiebert

To this point in our discussions, we primarily have dealt with the development of mentoring as a process in organizations and have attempted to tie the concept to the field of counseling. In addition, we have discussed the similarities and differences in mentoring among men, women, and members of underrepresented groups. Through these discussions, it has become apparent that there are at least three different components necessary for effective mentoring to occur, including career advancement, psychosocial issues, and role modeling. In this chapter, I discuss several types of mentoring programs and models, highlighting their applications to the field of counseling. Because all protégés may benefit from access to each of the essential components of mentoring, this chapter primarily focuses on programs and models that attempt to integrate all three components for effective mentoring regardless of the intended audience. Multiple mentoring, peer mentoring, and several sample mentoring programs are discussed.

Multiple Mentoring

The concept of multiple mentoring makes intuitive sense. In this model, protégés have more than one mentor and benefit from the strengths of each mentor. As previously discussed, men have benefited from the traditional model of mentoring but also have been shown to benefit from mentoring through involvement in a variety of professional networks and short-term collaborative efforts similar to mentoring. The multiple-mentoring model may work particularly well for women and members of other underrepresented groups by allowing them to benefit from the inclusion of several mentors rather than searching for the perfect mentor. In addition, individuals may find easier access to less intense mentoring relationships formed with several persons or groups who act as mentors. This is due to the fact that the mentor may feel less pressure to meet all of the protégé's mentoring needs if multiple mentors are involved.

It is important to note that the development of multiple mentoring relationships may occur as a result of either an informal process or a formal program. That is, a novice or potential protégé may choose to develop informal relationships with several mentors in order to meet his or her own mentoring needs. Conversely, or perhaps in addition to an informal mentoring strategy, an individual may participate in a formal multiple-mentoring program sponsored by an organization. These programs are designed and implemented by the organization to assist all junior members of the organization in their professional and personal development. These formal programs benefit both the organization and the employees.

There are several benefits associated with the multiple-mentoring model. The potential protégé may not waste time and effort looking for the perfect mentor. In addition, the potential protégé does not have to wait around for a mentor to recognize his or her talents and to initiate the mentoring relationship. This model allows the protégé to benefit from the advice and perspectives of several mentors rather than depending on one mentor's experiences. Additionally, the multiple-mentor model increases the probability that all three components of an effective mentoring relationship will be met by one or more of the mentors. Multiple-mentor models also increase the probability that the protégé may benefit from having male and female members from the same and different ethnic backgrounds and individuals from various positions in the organization as mentors. Finally, mentors may be more willing to engage in the mentoring process with protégés who have multiple mentors because both the mentors and the protégés realize that the investment of time and energy may be spread across mentors. This is particularly important when a specific individual is in high demand as a mentor (i.e., may be the only female faculty member, the only Hispanic male in the school, or the only individual with particular expertise in an organization).

Organizations also benefit from the multiple-mentoring model. Mentoring efforts are spread among employees and, therefore, take less time from potential mentors. Organizationally sponsored programs may result in fewer sexual dilemmas for male–female mentoring pairs. Furthermore, organizations may pair mentors and protégés on the basis of the protégés' developmental levels within the organizations. One mentor may provide assistance in learning the social structure of the organization, whereas another mentor may focus on the specific job tasks required of the protégé. Once these goals have been met, the protégé may move on to another mentoring relationship, in which he or she may learn skills and knowledge required for the next developmental level within the organization.

There are some negative aspects of the multiple-mentoring model. Some researchers argue that multiple-mentoring models never have the same power or influence on an individual and his or her career as a single, powerful, senior person. Furthermore, the intense interpersonal relationship that tends to develop between a single mentor and his or her protégé also may be missing from a multiple-mentor model. However, many would argue that a multiple-mentor model is less hierarchical in nature, may be more inclusive in nature, and may create a healthier and more supportive environment.

Burlew (1991) described a conceptual framework for the development of multiple-mentor programs. His model is based on the human resource development training model developed by Nadler (1979). Nadler's model was designed to help trainers provide appropriate training, education, and development activities for workers in organizations. It includes three stages: training, education, and development, each of which provides different activities and skills appropriate to a worker's particular developmental stage. Similarly, Burlew's model proposes three levels of mentoring: training mentor, education mentor, and development mentor.

The first level of mentoring in Burlew's (1991) model is the training mentor. The training mentor helps a worker make a successful adjustment to the work environment. The training mentor may be anyone who has knowledge of a particular job or certain job experience and who is willing to share that knowledge with a potential protégé. In this case, the training mentor would be part of a formal mentoring program. The training mentor also may be accessed through an informal network. For example, an older relative who gives a younger relative advice on how to behave in his or her first job may act in this capacity. This relative may offer advice related to adjusting to the work environment, such as arriving on time and always going above and beyond what you are asked to do. In both of these instances, either formal or informal, the protégé may have several training mentors, and they all may be assigned through the formal program, informal mentors, or a mixture of both.

Training mentors need to possess skills related to job coaching, instruction, and evaluation. Training mentors also must possess knowledge specifically related to working various jobs and adjusting to particular working environments. In addition, training mentors must provide a new worker with the guidance necessary to master the job, assist the protégé in acclimating to the work environment, support the protégé until he or she develops a sense of competence, and suggest opportunities to help the protégé advance and become a more valuable employee.

The second level of mentoring in Burlew's (1991) model of multiple mentoring is that of education mentor. The mentor (or mentors) in this stage provides the protégé with information related to career opportunities and advancement either within the organization or with a new organization. Specifically, the education mentor helps the protégé plan for the future, make decisions about education and work, succeed in spite of difficulty, develop strong support groups, and develop the necessary skills to succeed. The education mentor must possess good helping skills and have a good knowledge of the world of work. Education mentors may include career counselors, human resource personnel, relatives, or successful senior employees in a particular field.

The third level of mentoring in Burlew's (1991) model is that of development mentor. This is a unique individual who assists the protégé in identifying and engaging in activities that may benefit the organization and the protégé in the future. The development mentor helps the protégé grow as a person and move toward personal and professional self-actualization. The development mentor may help the protégé assess personal strengths and weaknesses, develop plans of action for change, develop unexplored talents, network, and ultimately realize and reach his or her potential. The development mentor may be an individual who has attained a certain level of self-actualization. This person may be a career counselor, an individual counselor, a human resource development specialist, or a successful senior employee in a particular field.

Burlew's (1991) model has several implications for counselors, including implications for individual counseling, school counseling, training, and research. Furthermore, the model provides potential opportunities for the protégé to experience mentoring in the areas of career advancement, psychosocial development, and role modeling. The protégé may engage multiple mentors at each level of mentoring and simultaneously engage multiple mentors across levels, depending on the individual circumstances. In addition, the multiple-mentor model provides opportunities for informal mentoring at each level and for organizations to create mentoring opportunities and to provide training for mentors at each level.

Finally, Burlew's (1991) multiple-mentor model provides excellent examples of how counselors may serve as mentors to their clients. For example, counselors may serve as mentors by acting as role models for their clients. This has been a controversial topic, with some experts suggesting that it is inappropriate for counselors to act as mentors for their clients. These critics suggest that this situation may lead to difficulties with boundaries and with dual-role relationships. On the contrary, this model allows counselors to appropriately define how counselors may serve as mentors for their clients and why many clients identify their counselors as mentors.

Peer Mentoring

Peer mentoring programs are designed to help individuals at the same level within organizations learn from each other. For example, 2nd-year counseling students may form mentoring relationships with 1st-year counseling students. Fourth-grade students may form mentoring relationships with 1st-grade students. In Alcoholics Anonymous, beginning members are paired with sober members (sponsors) to form mentoring relationships. In this way, individuals who are merely further along in some respect but who are members of the same group within an organization work together. Peer mentoring programs have been successfully implemented in a variety of settings, including universities, elementary and secondary schools, community organizations, and business and industry (Goodlad, 1996). These programs are largely based on a more formal mentoring program structure and are designed and implemented by community and school counselors, counselor educators, educational psychologists, and business leaders, to name but a few.

The use of peer mentoring programs has several advantages over traditional mentoring approaches. Perhaps most important, peer mentoring in educational settings allows the peer mentors to reach where neither the teacher nor any adult could otherwise reach (Topping, 1996). These findings may be extrapolated to other settings. For example, 2nd-year counselor education students in mentoring programs with new counselor education students may develop relationships that address issues that faculty mentors and protégés may never discuss. In addition, the perspectives of the more advanced student mentors may provide valuable insights to the protégés that the faculty mentors could not. Other examples of the value of peer mentoring include those seen in community programs, such as Alcoholics Anonymous, in which sponsors mentor and reach new members in ways that others, even professional helpers, may not be able to.

Other advantages of peer mentoring programs include the opportunity for peer mentors to provide mentoring in each of the three areas previously identified: career and educational advancement, psychosocial issues, and role modeling. The opportunity for the protégé to identify directly with the mentor may be much stronger in peer mentoring relationships because of the relative lack of hierarchical structure and because of the relatively recent experience of the mentor in the protégé's current position. This identification may give the mentor more credibility and influence and may establish him or her as a powerful role model.

Peer mentoring programs provide advantages for the mentors as well. These benefits include a sense of self-confidence and self-esteem, an awareness and responsibility related to helping others, a feeling of giving something back, and a deeper sense of understanding their own experience through the mentoring process. Peer mentoring also provides opportunities for both parties to gain better interpersonal skills and form networks among peers.

Disadvantages of peer mentoring are also evident. Peer mentors may portray their experience as the typical experience to the protégé. This may or may not be positive and may or may not be accurate. Peer mentors may find that they lack appropriate helping skills. Therefore, it is important that they are familiar with sources of referral and individuals who may provide consultation. Confidentiality also may be a problem in peer mentoring relationships. Finally, if used exclusively, peer mentoring does not provide the protégé with access to mentors in higher positions within the community or organization who may have the power and influence to help the protégé advance both personally and professionally.

Peer mentoring programs have been developed and implemented in a variety of settings, and several excellent models are described in the literature. Some of the key elements for success in peer mentoring programs include appropriately selecting peer mentors, training peer mentors to provide them with necessary knowledge and skills, and providing peer mentors with backup assistance for themselves and their mentees. Written guidelines and role-playing exercises also may be particularly beneficial in the training of peer mentors.

Because peer mentoring programs may be developed in a multitude of settings and should be individualized to the setting and population, readers are referred to additional sources for programs specific to populations and settings of interest. For a more complete review of the effectiveness of school peer mentoring programs developed nationally and internationally, see Goodlad (1996) and Topping (1988). For more information regarding community self-help programs in which peer mentoring is used, the reader is referred to those programs. In addition, literature documenting the effectiveness of peer mentoring programs can be found in the literature specific to those particular fields.

Combined Approaches to Mentoring

Combined approaches to mentoring seek to use formal and informal methods of mentoring to provide a comprehensive mentoring program. In a sample combined mentoring program at the State University of New York College at Cortland, three strategies were used (Hall, 1983). First, a course was developed that exposed female students to nontraditional career options, raised their awareness about career options and lifestyles, and discussed modes of entry into nontraditional and traditional occupations. Second, protégés were exposed to guest speakers who acted as role models by discussing their careers and professional as well as personal issues. The third component involved one-on-one interaction between faculty mentors and student protégés.

The combined approach to mentoring allows opportunities for discussion related to career advancement and psychosocial issues and provides opportunities for role modeling. This approach could easily be modified for counselor education programs, elementary and secondary school mentoring programs, and community–school–business mentoring partnerships.

Mentoring Partnerships

Another model of mentoring that has grown in popularity in the recent past is a model based on the establishment of mentoring partnerships. Mentoring partnerships may be formed between and among universities, schools, community programs, and private-sector companies. One example of a mentoring partnership involves a high school, professionals in the community, and a nearby college. In this program, high school students who had been identified as being at risk for failure or dropping out of school were invited to join the mentoring program. Students were then surveyed to ascertain areas of vocational and personal interest. They were then paired with mentors from the community who had volunteered to work in the program and who had expressed similar interests. These mentors served as role models for the students, provided them with information regarding career and educational options, and provided them with encouragement. In addition to the professional mentor, the student was paired with a volunteer college student who was majoring in the high school student's expressed area of interest. The college student also served as a role model, provided information, and encouraged the student to work toward his or her goals.

This mentoring program, based on multiple mentoring partnerships, provided at-risk students with opportunities to access different types of mentors. In this way, students were exposed to professionals in the community who were already successfully working in the protégés' interest areas. In addition, students were exposed to another perspective when working with the college student mentors. This program has been very successful in helping students remain in high school and in encouraging these students to pursue higher education. The program also has assisted the protégés in making a successful transition from high school to postsecondary education.

Other programs based on mentoring partnerships include community-based programs such as Big Brothers/Big Sisters, Adopt a Grandparent, and Junior Achievement. In these programs, volunteers from the community are paired with an individual student or work with a group of students to provide skill development and encouragement and to enhance self-esteem. These mentors act as role models to their protégés and provide them with exposure to career and lifestyle options that they otherwise might never experience.

An example of this type of program is the Across Ages Program, sponsored by Temple University's Center for Intergenerational

Learning. This program is an intergenerational approach to drug prevention for high-risk middle school students. The project was designed to increase the resiliency and protective factors within youth in five domains: the individual, the family, the school, the peer group, and the community (LoScuito, Rajala, Townsend, & Taylor, 1996).

The basis of the program is the establishment of a mentoring relationship between older adult volunteers (ages 55 and older) and high-risk middle school students. Older mentors help these children develop awareness, self-confidence, and skills they need to resist drugs by acting as advocates, challengers, nurturers, role models, and friends. In addition to the mentor pairings, the program engages students in community service activities that benefit older persons, provides a classroom-based life-skills curriculum, and offers workshops to parents (LoScuito et al., 1996).

This mentoring partnership provides benefits for the students as well as the older mentors. Older mentors are an untapped resource in the United States. In addition, according to Erikson (1960), generativity is an important life task to older persons. Through the process of mentoring, older persons may achieve a sense of generativity, that is, a feeling of transmitting one's knowledge and experience to the next generation.

Older mentors are carefully recruited, screened, trained, and matched with high-risk students. These mentors then receive supervision from project staff throughout their participation in the program. Most mentors are on a fixed income and receive a small monthly stipend (approximately $60) to make it possible for them to volunteer. Each mentor spends approximately 4 hours a week with his or her protégé, engaging in a variety of activities such as helping with homework, attending sporting or cultural events, or participating in community service together. Mentors meet with their protégés throughout the year, even during the summer, which can be an especially difficult time for protégés.

A classic randomized pretest–posttest control group design was used to evaluate this program's effectiveness (LoScuito et al., 1996). The results of this evaluation indicated that the mentors may have provided an extra benefit to the students by helping them develop coping and resistance skills regarding alcohol, tobacco, and other drug use. In addition, the group that participated in the mentoring component seemed to have a better attendance record than those groups without mentoring. Students with mentors reported more positive attitudes toward school, their future, older people, and participation in community service. Results of the evaluation also indicated that mentoring may be effective in increasing students' reported sense of self-worth, promoting feelings of well-being, and reducing feelings of sadness and loneliness, as well as discouraging use of various substances.

The results of this study are supported by other findings in the literature related to the effectiveness of community and school mentoring partnerships (Dondero, 1997). The possibilities for developing these types of mentoring partnerships are numerous and may be tailored to the needs and resources of a particular community. Both school and community counselors may be instrumental in developing and implementing these types of mentoring programs in their schools and communities. In addition, counselor educators may use mentoring partnerships between local high schools, undergraduate institutions, and community organizations to recruit underrepresented students into counseling programs. Given the effectiveness of mentoring partnership programs and the reduced ability of counselors to see clients in individual sessions for long periods of time, it is important that counselor educators and counselors working across settings be familiar with the benefits of these programs. Mentoring programs may be implemented to maximize resources and to benefit mentors and protégés. For further information on developing school–community partnerships, see Dondero (1997).

Paper Mentors

An interesting alternative to traditional mentoring includes paper mentoring. In this type of mentoring, protégés may benefit from publications that give "how to" and "how not to" advice. For example, in *Counseling Today,* there is a column titled "Finding Your Way," and in the *Chronicle of Higher Education,* there is a column that provides specific advice on commonly asked career-type questions and career etiquette that may be considered a paper-mentoring resource. Paper-mentoring resources may be developed by institutions, departments, professional associations, or individuals. Often they are designed by and targeted toward members of particular audiences, such as women (Hall, 1983). Examples of these resources include such books as *A Handbook for Women Scholars* (Spencer, Kehoe, & Speece, 1982) and *What to Do Until the Mentor Arrives* (Moore, 1982).

Other paper mentors are geared toward more general audiences and are useful across disciplines. Examples of these resources include such books as *What Color Is Your Parachute?* (Bolles, 1999) and *How to Get a Job* (Bert, 1974).

Although some may argue that paper mentors are not really mentors at all, this type of mentoring may be readily available when more traditional forms of mentoring are not. Instead of encouraging individuals to wait for that perfect mentor to come along, these resources may provide critical information until one can take advantage of other forms of mentoring. In addition, this form of mentoring can be used to supplement more traditional forms of mentoring in much the same way that bibliotherapy can be used to supplement more traditional forms of counseling.

Career Cooperatives as Mentoring Alternatives

Career cooperatives (sometimes called "job clubs") consist of individuals who meet regularly to assist members in developing advancement skills and by sharing information and contacts related to the job market. These career cooperatives provide avenues for mutual support for individuals who are building careers. Members support each other and build personal and professional networks across institutions, professions, and generations. These career cooperatives may provide links to senior-level professionals or may invite senior-level professionals to be guest speakers. These speakers provide members with information on the political and social aspects of the profession and competencies needed to deal successfully with them.

As with the other mentoring programs discussed in this chapter, specific activities undertaken in career cooperatives will vary with the discipline, organizational setting, and needs of individual members. However, group discussion and group facilitation are essential components of all successful career cooperatives. Skills and topics to be included in the development of the career cooperatives include three broad areas: skills involved in getting a first position or subsequent positions, competencies necessary for maintaining one's position, and competencies for moving up the career ladder. Topics in each of these areas are presented in such a way as to engage all members of the group in skill-building exercises, such as asking group members to critique each other's resumes or to role-play to practice interviewing skills. Another means of engaging group members may include promoting discussion of important topics, such as how to negotiate a job offer, how to establish new contacts, or how to identify potential mentors.

These career cooperatives may not seem to the reader to fall into the same category as more traditional approaches; however, on further examination, one may see that this type of mentoring alternative potentially does provide members with career advancement strategies, psychosocial support, and exposure to role models. Career counselors, vocational rehabilitation counselors, and employee assistance counselors may consider career cooperatives as ways to enhance mentoring activities and make them more accessible to those individuals who may benefit from them the most. In addition, this type of mentoring program may help maximize resources while at the same time providing many of the benefits associated with more traditional mentoring.

Conclusion

Several different types of mentoring programs have been discussed in this chapter. Each has its strengths and limitations, and each must be individually developed and implemented on the basis of the particular setting and individuals involved. Most of the programs discussed in this chapter may be designed to meet career advancement needs, psychosocial needs, and role-modeling needs for potential protégés.

It is important to note that participation in one type of mentoring program does not necessarily mean that one may not benefit from participating in a variety of different mentoring experiences. The programs discussed in this chapter represent, for the most part, more formal types of mentoring. That is, they are designed as mentoring programs sponsored by an organization, through which mentors and protégés are matched according to some criteria for preestablished purposes. This is in contrast to more informal mentoring relationships that occur spontaneously between mentor and protégé on the basis of mutual definition.

Perhaps the most beneficial mentoring occurs when individuals have access to both formal and informal mentoring relationships. In this way, individuals may have access to specific knowledge and opportunities sanctioned by the organization and may benefit from a more intimate, personal mentoring relationship formed sponta-neously between mentor and protégé. The following chapter fo-cuses on the mentoring strategies that may be used to facilitate the development, maintenance, and termination of these more informal mentoring relationships.

References

Bert, F. (1974). *How to get a job.* Homewood, IL: ETC Publications.

Bolles, R. N. (1999). *What color is your parachute?* Berkeley, CA: Ten Speed Press.

Burlew, L. (1991). Multiple mentor model: A conceptual framework. *Journal of Career Development, 17,* 213–221.

Dondero, G. (1997). Mentors: Beacons of hope. *Adolescence, 32,* 881–886.

Erikson, E. (1960). *Identity and the lifecycle.* New York: International Univer-sities Press.

Goodlad, S. (1996). *Students as tutors and mentors.* London: Kogan Page.

Hall, R. (1983). *Academic mentoring for women students and faculty: A new look at an old way to get ahead.* Washington, DC: Project on the Status and Ed-ucation of Women, Association of American Colleges.

LoScuito, L., Rajala, A., Townsend, T., & Taylor, A. (1996). An outcome evaluation of Across Ages: An intergenerational mentoring approach to drug prevention. *Journal of Adolescent Research, 11,* 116–129.

Moore, K. M. (1982). *What to do until the mentor arrives?* Washington, DC: National Association for Women Deans, Administrators and Coun-selors.

Nadler, L. (1979). *Developing human resources* (2nd ed.). Austin, TX: Learning Concepts.

Spencer, M. L., Kehoe, M., & Speece, K. (1982). *Handbook for women scholars: Strategies for success.* San Francisco: Center for Women Scholars, Amer-ica's Behavioral Research Corporation.

Topping, K. J. (1988). *The peer tutoring handbook.* London: Croom Helm.

Topping, K. J. (1996). Reaching where adults cannot: Peer education and peer counseling. *Educational Psychology, 11*(4), 23–29.

7

Mentoring Strategies

By Valerie L. Schwiebert

*I*n the preceding chapter, several examples of formal mentoring programs were presented and discussed. The focus of this chapter is on strategies used by mentors and protégés to initiate, develop, sustain, and ultimately terminate effective mentoring relationships. More specifically, roles of mentors and protégés are examined; effective strategies for mentors and protégés are proposed; developmental phases of the informal mentoring relationship are discussed; and, finally, strategies for evaluating the effectiveness of individual mentoring strategies are given.

Mentoring can assume a variety of structures, as described in various chapters throughout this book. Examples of these structures include formal and informal mentoring, short- and long-term mentoring, cross-gender mentoring, multicultural mentoring, and peer mentoring (Shea, 1992). The strategies described below may be used across mentoring structures to enhance the mentoring relationship between mentor and protégé.

Roles of Mentors

Mentoring programs vary among institutions and between settings. Some mentoring programs are formal, to the degree of assigned pairings, whereas others are totally products of individual inclinations. Regardless of the parameters of any given institutional mentoring program, there are common obligations and responsibilities associated with acting as a mentor. These common roles are discussed in this section.

Mentors may be called on to fill a variety of roles in the mentoring relationship. As previously discussed, psychosocial issues, career development, and role modeling are the three primary components in a successful mentoring relationship. These components may include specific mentor roles in each area. Mentor roles that may be fulfilled in the psychosocial component include modeling competence and identity, encouraging risk taking, providing the protégé with acceptance and validation, serving as a confidant and friend, and assisting the protégé in developing a social network. These roles focus on shaping the personal development of the protégé, making a relational connection with the protégé, and assisting the protégé in developing a sense of self as a professional (Kram, 1985).

Roles associated with the career development component of mentoring include sponsorship, promotion, exposure, visibility, coaching, and protection. Mentors also may give protégés assignments that increase visibility and competence, showcasing the protégé's talents (Galbraith & Cohen, 1995). These roles focus more on organizational structure and building a relationship within the roles and norms of the institution.

Finally, mentors serve as role models for their protégés (Kram, 1985). As role models, mentors provide protégés with opportunities to experience and learn various approaches to survival in the organization through observation. As the protégé observes the actions and interactions of the mentor, he or she integrates those approaches that seem most beneficial and discards those that either seem ineffective or do not fit the protégé's style.

In addition to serving in various roles, the mentor provides the protégé with specific benefits and opportunities. These include providing the protégé with opportunities for recognition and encouragement, honest feedback, advice on balancing responsibilities, and knowledge of the informal rules of the organization. They also address appropriate ways of making contact with senior members of the organization, information on professional behavior, skills for showcasing one's own work, advice on developing networks, and a perspective on long-term career planning (Shea, 1992). Mentors also use their own connections and contacts to involve the protégé in joint projects and research, introduce the protégé to top authorities in the field, nominate the protégé for awards and recognition, and support the protégé for promotion. Finally, the protégé may benefit indirectly from the reflected power of the mentor. That is, because the mentor is usually a powerful and respected member of the organization, the protégé frequently enjoys a special status and acceptance through association with the mentor (Ragins & McFarlin, 1990).

Roles of Protégés

Protégés may prepare themselves for successful mentoring experiences from the outset. The organization may or may not have a formal mentoring program. This will influence, to some degree, the nature of the mentoring relationship. However, there are some common characteristics that protégés in successful mentoring relationships display. Strategies for actively seeking and engaging in successful mentoring relationships are discussed in this section.

Protégés also must take an active role in the mentoring relationship. First, protégés must assume full responsibility for their own development. An essential component of active participation is asking for what one needs (Daresh & Playko, 1995). Therefore, protégés must continually assess their strengths, weaknesses, goals, and progress. Then the protégés may engage in a dialogue with the mentors that is open and concrete. Remaining open and receptive to new ideas and feedback is also an important role for the protégés so that they will receive maximum benefit from the mentoring relationship. Finally, the protégés need to recognize the time and effort given by the mentors and express appreciation for the assistance given. This means not only verbally acknowledging the assistance given by the mentors but also exhibiting professional behavior that respects the mentors' time and commitment. Professional behaviors include keeping appointments, arriving on time, following through on commitments, respecting the mentors' boundaries, and communicating difficulties and successes to the mentors.

Mentor Strategies for Establishing and Maintaining Effective Mentoring Relationships

Once an individual has agreed to be a mentor, several strategies may be beneficial in establishing mutually beneficial and effective mentoring relationships. First, both mentor and protégé must decide what knowledge, skills, strengths, and weaknesses they bring to the relationship. It is particularly important for the mentor to recognize what he or she may offer the protégé, realizing he or she does not have to fill every mentoring function for the protégé. The protégé also must be able to articulate his or her needs and hopes for the mentoring relationship.

It may be helpful for both parties to develop a written document or to engage in a discussion of the expectations that mentor and protégé hold for the relationship. This may prevent future misunderstandings and may allow both parties to fully understand the commitment they are making to the relationship. It also may be helpful in managing the relationship if one party begins to ask for too much time and energy or has too little commitment in the relationship. This degree of formality may not always be necessary or desirable; however, it may prevent mentor and protégé from entering into the relationship with different expectations that never become known until one or both parties are dissatisfied with the relationship. Even in a more informal relationship, discussions should occur between mentor and protégé that include topics such as when and how often meetings will occur and particular expectations that each individual has for what will occur in these meetings and as a result of the mentoring relationship.

Once the mentor and the protégé have entered into the mentoring relationship, either formally or informally, there are several strategies that the mentor may use to assist the protégé. First, it is important that the mentor recognizes his or her strengths, contacts, and resources. Many potential mentors never engage in mentoring relationships, or never identify relationships as mentoring, because they underestimate the potential contributions they can make to their protégés (Ragins & Cotton, 1993). A good mentor is not necessarily someone who is at the top of his or her field. As previously discussed, a mentor may be from the same population and at a different developmental level than the protégé or even a peer mentor.

Mentors need to clarify their expectations of protégés. This is important for both mentor and protégé. If the mentor's expectations are too high, the protégé may become discouraged. If the mentor's expectations are too low, the protégé may not receive maximum benefit from the relationship. One strategy that may assist mentors in clarifying their expectations of protégés is for them to think about their own careers and achievements and to decide if they are basing their expectations on their own accomplishments or on the potentials of their protégés.

Mentors also should set aside time to spend with their protégés. It is important for the mentor to keep scheduled appointments and to be accessible to the protégé. This demonstrates the mentor's commitment to the mentoring relationship and models good professional behavior. The mentor also needs to maintain good boundaries with the protégé, establishing appropriate times and places for contact to occur. For example, is it appropriate for the protégé to contact the mentor at home? If so, when, how often, and until what time is this appropriate? The mentor may need to provide specific guidance to the protégé regarding such matters.

Another essential component of the mentoring relationship is the provision of constructive feedback to the protégé. The mentor should be certain he or she provides both positive and negative feedback. This feedback should always be specific and given in private, in a setting that is as nonthreatening as possible. Mentors should be sensitive to their position and to the weight that their comments may carry for the protégés. When providing feedback, mentors should allow protégés to respond and then brainstorm strategies for correcting the identified problems. It may be helpful for the mentor to remember that providing support and encouragement is also an essential component of the mentoring relationship and this component should be balanced with constructive feedback (Shea, 1992).

Another important strategy for the mentor to use is that of sponsorship, that is, helping the protégé connect to professional and personal networks and making sure the protégé's accomplishments are noticed. This involves introducing the protégé to colleagues and other important individuals; nominating the protégé for committees and other assignments; and including the protégé in appropriate meetings, projects, and social events. In addition, the mentor should take every opportunity to showcase the protégé's work and accomplishments. This may be done during informal meetings, conferences, and professional association meetings both inside and outside of one's organization. Ultimately, the mentor may assist the protégé in accessing these networks to obtain a new position. The mentor may advise the protégé of open positions, write letters of recommendation for the protégé, and serve as a reference for the protégé.

The mentor also should include the protégé in informal activities such as lunches, discussions following meetings, and receptions at conferences. In this way, the protégé can learn the social expectations of individuals in a particular field, meet other protégés and professionals in the field, gain recognition among his or her colleagues, and build his or her own networks (Shea, 1992).

Informal activities also may be important for the mentor and the protégé. During these times, the mentor may provide feedback, support, and encouragement for the protégé in nonthreatening environments. These activities also may strengthen the mentoring relationship and provide the protégé with opportunities to discuss issues at a different level than meetings in a more formal environment.

Another essential strategy for mentors to use when working with their protégés is educating protégés regarding available resources and institutional support. Mentors may encourage and assist protégés in writing grants, seeking funds for attending workshops and other training, gaining access to education reimbursement programs, and helping protégés seek release time for special projects. Mentors also may use resources available to them to provide protégés with access to those same resources that might otherwise be unavailable to the protégés. Technology, library access, research support, photocopying, laptop computers, and labs are examples of such resources.

Another important component of the mentoring relationship that the mentor provides is protecting the protégé from making costly career and personal mistakes. That is, the mentor may make the protégé aware of things that might reflect negatively on him or her. This may be accomplished by problem solving with the protégé to help him or her examine the consequences of differing courses of action and choose the best option. An additional form of protection that a mentor may provide is protecting the protégé from becoming overextended and not being able to give his or her best to assignments (Galbraith & Cohen, 1995).

Finally, perhaps one of the most important strategies for effective mentoring is active listening. Mentors should provide opportunities for protégés to express frustrations, share accomplishments, discuss problems, and set goals. Although mentoring does involve giving advice regarding career and other decisions, the effective mentor acts as a sounding board, providing options and information for the protégé, normalizing experiences and feelings, assisting the protégé in resolving crises, and facilitating the development of plans based on the protégé's goals. In many instances, the mentor may find that all the protégé really needs is for someone who has been there to listen, affirm, and understand.

Protégé Strategies for Establishing and Maintaining Effective Mentoring Relationships

Protégés must take an active part in identifying and developing mentoring relationships. First, protégés must decide if they need a mentor and, if so, what type of mentoring relationship would be most beneficial. Depending on the organizational setting, protégés may ask themselves several questions: Who are the important people in the organization? Who has direct relationships with these individuals? How do people in the organization or field find out about opportunities for advancement? How do people in the organization or field get nominated for positions, awards, and recognition? What professional organizations or conferences are the most important? How do people in the field find out about job openings? What types of experiences are most important to obtain and to have in one's vita? What are the social rules of the organization (e.g., appropriate ways to raise concerns)? What type of sponsorship would be most beneficial to the individual? What issues does the individual want or need assistance in working through?

If the protégé can identify specific areas in which a mentor may be helpful, then the next step is to identify a potential mentor. A number of factors may influence the protégé's decision to identify a particular potential mentor. The first question should be, What individuals in the organization or community demonstrate or possess the needed skills, knowledge, or expertise? What are the committees, panels, or organizations to which the individual belongs? What is he or she known for in the field or organization? Is the individual recognized nationally or internationally outside of the organization? What influence does the individual have in the organization and field? Does the individual set high standards for himself or herself? (Shea, 1992).

Once a potential pool of mentors has been identified, the protégé must decide which of these individuals to approach regarding a mentoring relationship. The protégé must consider whom he or she may work well with both personally and professionally. Is the mentor someone who has indicated an interest in and support of the protégé? Does the individual already have several protégés? What has happened to this individual's former protégés? Does the person seem to work equally well with male and female protégés? Is the individual someone who would be able to understand the protégé's views, needs, and goals? Does the individual possess good interpersonal skills that allow him or her to give advice and direction? Does the individual's work seem to be viewed favorably in the institution and by coworkers? Does the individual have a good network, and will he or she refer the protégé if he or she does not have the necessary answers or resources?

After considering each of these areas, the protégé may choose to use several strategies to obtain the mentor he or she has identified. Protégés may actively seek mentors, rather than waiting passively for someone to notice their achievements and choose them. First, the protégé should introduce himself or herself. This can be accomplished in several ways. The protégé may speak to the person after a class, meeting, or presentation. The protégé may write the potential mentor a letter or memo asking a question in relation to a professional subject. The protégé also may send the senior person a draft of a paper or other work and request the potential mentor's feedback and comments.

The protégé may begin to ask the potential mentor for feedback regarding strengths and weaknesses of his or her work. It is important that the protégé be prepared to express appreciation for advice and criticism. This will provide the mentor with an opportunity to become familiar with the protégé's work and to observe the protégé's willingness to respond to constructive feedback.

The protégé may attempt to become a research assistant, junior collaborator, intern, or other type of apprentice. This will provide the protégé with an opportunity to receive feedback and instruction, which would naturally occur and which may then evolve into a mentoring relationship. In addition, this type of work will give the protégé an opportunity to demonstrate his or her abilities and commitment.

The protégé may ask colleagues who have relationships with the potential mentor to mention his or her name to the mentor. In addition, the protégé may volunteer to serve on a taskforce or a committee on which the potential mentor is also a member. If the protégé chooses to do this, then taking on a significant assignment that will require significant collaboration may be particularly beneficial.

Finally, once the protégé has made an effort to bring his or her work to the attention of the mentor, the protégé may wish to directly approach the potential mentor. In this case, the protégé may schedule an appointment with the potential mentor and discuss his or her request that the individual serve in the capacity of mentor. If the mentor declines to serve in this capacity, the protégé may ask the mentor to recommend someone else who may be able to serve in the mentoring capacity. If no recommendations are forthcoming, the protégé may try innovative strategies such as hiring someone to provide specific mentoring advice, knowledge, skills, and information or using paper mentors.

Once the mentoring relationship has been established and goals have been set, the protégé must follow through on his or her commitments, going above and beyond what is required. It is important that the protégé always bear in mind that the ultimate goal of the mentoring relationship is to promote and develop the protégé's best efforts. Giving one's best in every undertaking will serve to maximize the potential benefits for the protégé. The protégé also should take advantage of all opportunities provided by the mentor. For example, if the mentor invites the protégé to attend a professional meeting, the protégé should make every effort to attend. At the meeting, the protégé should actively make contacts, network, and engage others in professional discussions. This highlights the fact that the mentor can provide opportunities, but if the protégé does not do his or her part, then the benefits of the mentoring relationship will not be realized.

It is also important for the protégé to realize when he or she has outgrown the mentoring relationship. This can be accomplished by continually evaluating one's goals and progress toward those goals with the mentor. In this way, both mentor and protégé can see when the goals have been reached and when the mentoring relationship is no longer beneficial. At that time, the protégé also must take an active role in acknowledging the assistance of the mentor and renegotiating the relationship.

Phases of the Mentoring Relationship

Development of the mentoring relationship can be divided into four stages (Galbraith & Cohen, 1995). The first stage is initiation. In this stage, the focus is on building rapport, establishing trust, and developing realistic expectations. During the initiation stage, the mentor may gain satisfaction from being actively sought after for his or her advice and counsel. The protégé also may gain satisfaction and a sense of importance from the mentor's attention. Also during this stage, the parameters of the mentoring relationship are established and agreed on.

The cultivation stage is the second stage of the mentoring relationship. During this stage, mentor and protégé have settled into a comfortable working relationship. This stage is often characterized by feelings of stability and mutual satisfaction. The focus is on making progress toward the goals set in the development stage.

The third phase of the mentoring relationship is the separation stage. In this stage, the focus is on ending the mentoring relationship in an amicable manner. This is the point at which formal mentoring ends. This may be due to the protégé having outgrown the mentor's ability to provide productive guidance. It may be a mutual decision, or one party may decide it is time to terminate the mentoring relationship.

The final stage of the mentoring relationship is redefinition. This is a critical stage for mentoring and one that is often neglected. During this stage, the relationship between the individuals is redefined, and both individuals must adjust to the new relationship. In many instances, the individuals in this new relationship begin to relate to one another as friends, peers, and colleagues. In a few instances, the relationship may not continue if the separation is particularly difficult and not a mutual decision.

It is important to note that protégé and mentor have equal responsibilities for making the mentoring relationship work at each stage. The mentor may provide opportunities, but the protégé must take them. Likewise, the mentor must recognize when the protégé has reached a point at which the mentor may no longer provide the kind of assistance the protégé needs. At that point, mentor and protégé must work to redefine their own relationship and to connect the protégé with other mentors who may be able to meet his or her needs.

Mentoring Strategies and Counseling

Many of the strategies that are used in effective counseling are applicable to establishing and maintaining effective mentoring relationships. Counseling is based on establishing a helping relationship by utilizing skills such as active listening, rapport building, goal identification, goal setting, action planning, and termination. Mentoring strategies involve using the same types of skills to establish the relationship, set goals, take action, and then terminate the relationship. Likewise, the ultimate goal of counseling is to help clients become independent of the counselor, to solve problems on their own, and to generalize what they have learned to similar situations. The ultimate goal of the mentoring relationship is to promote the protégé's career and personal growth so that the protégé no longer needs the mentor's help, can function independently using the skills learned from the mentor, and can terminate and renegotiate the relationship.

Additional parallels between the mentoring relationship and the counseling relationship include a focus on the needs of the protégé or the client, respectively. In the counseling relationship, the client's welfare is of utmost priority. In the mentoring relationship, the protégé's welfare must be of utmost priority to the mentor. This means that the mentor should not use the mentoring relationship to further his or her own career at the expense of the protégé. Examples include taking credit for work actually done by the protégé, guiding a protégé in a particular course of action to further the mentor's career, or holding onto the mentoring relationship when it no longer is benefiting the protégé.

Because counselors and counselor educators possess many of the skills needed for building effective mentoring relationships, they are in excellent positions to serve as mentors and to teach others to serve as mentors. As discussed in the previous chapter on mentoring programs, school and community counselors may be asked to develop and implement formal mentoring programs. Counselors may use their own education and background in counseling to teach potential peer and volunteer mentors strategies for building and maintaining effective mentoring relationships. Basic helping skills may be taught to potential mentors. Active listening and basic communication skills may be taught to both protégés and mentors to increase the effectiveness of the mentoring relationship. Counselors also may teach potential mentors strategies such as establishing and maintaining good boundaries, journaling, goal setting, problem solving, and decision making, all of which are applicable to the mentoring relationship.

Counselor educators also may draw on their counseling skills to develop positive mentoring relationships with counseling students. Counselor educators model appropriate mentoring strategies and discuss differences between counseling and mentoring with students. In addition, senior counseling students may be encouraged to act as mentors to new counseling students. Thus, they develop their own mentoring skills, which they may be called on to use in mentoring peers, mentoring in their work setting, or developing formal mentoring programs.

Conclusion

In conclusion, the discussion in this chapter has focused on the roles of mentors and protégés. Attempts were made to suggest strategies to be used by mentors and protégés in establishing, maintaining, terminating, and renegotiating mentoring relationships. Although many of these strategies will need to be tailored to the particular setting and mentoring relationship, they highlight the mutual responsibility shared by mentor and protégé for the failure or success of the relationship.

In addition, counselors and counselor educators possess unique knowledge and skills that may allow them to develop effective mentoring relationships with protégés, peers, and senior personnel to benefit themselves and others. These skills also may be used to develop and implement mentoring programs for use in counselor education programs and in the workplace. Therefore, it is essential that counselors and counselor educators begin to recognize and harness the power of mentoring to make a difference in their own lives, their students' lives, and the lives of their clients.

Throughout the chapters in this book, case examples of various mentoring experiences are included. Consider the strategies in this chapter and others that come to mind while reading the case examples. The reader is encouraged to reflect on how using some of the active strategies to enhance mentoring relationships presented in this chapter may have influenced the case examples as well as real-life experiences of the reader, if they had been implemented.

References

Daresh, J. C., & Playko, M. A. (1995, April). *Mentoring in education leadership development: What are the responsibilities of the protégés?* Paper presented at the meeting of the American Educational Research Association, San Francisco.

Galbraith, M., & Cohen, N. (1995). *Mentoring: New strategies and challenges.* San Francisco: Jossey-Bass.

Kram, K. E. (1985). *Mentoring at work.* Glenview, IL: Scott, Foresman.

Ragins, R. B., & Cotton, J. L. (1993). Gender and willingness to mentor in organizations. *Journal of Management, 19,* 97–111.

Ragins, R. B., & McFarlin, D. B. (1990). Perceptions of mentor roles in cross gender mentoring relationships. *Journal of Vocational Behavior, 37,* 321–339.

Shea, G. (1992). *Mentoring: A practical guide.* Menlo Park, CA: Crisp.

CHAPTER

8

The Role of Mentoring in the Professional Development of Counselors

By Cathy Woodyard

The preceding chapters have focused on an examination of the mentoring process drawn from research across disciplines. In this chapter, the role of mentoring in the professional development of counselors is discussed. Examples of topics included in the discussion are counseling faculty mentoring students, 2nd-year counseling students mentoring beginning counseling students, senior counseling faculty mentoring junior counseling faculty, and practicing counselors mentoring beginning counselors.

Throughout the developmental process that one goes through in becoming a professional counselor, various struggles, challenges, and crises are encountered. Whether one is a counselor-in-training, a new faculty member in a counselor education program, or a practicing counselor, professional development is an ongoing and evolving process. Having the benefit of a more experienced counselor as a mentor to assist in movement through this process can be an invaluable personal and professional resource.

Faculty Mentoring Students

I met my mentor through a course she taught titled "Life 101." The class drew from multicultural music, stories, and traditions worldwide. It actively engaged me in thinking deeply about living the fullest life I can.

> Previous to this class, I had decided to pursue an elementary education program in graduate school. However, during a "Life" class timed-writing exercise, I discovered that my true career passion was counseling. I wasn't interested in teaching academic subject matter. Instead, I wanted to help with children's emotional and mental well being. My mentor taught me many life lessons, such as the importance of having a vision, taking risks, getting out of my comfort zone, reaming from failure, and listening to my intuition. These continue to offer guidance in my journey to do what I love. (R. Arnsperger, personal communication, October 20, 1998)

The primary setting for professional development mentoring to occur for counselors is graduate school (Swerdlik & Bardon, 1988), and the experience described by Arnsperger is not unlike that of many counseling students. Mentoring is a process that occurs to aid and assist one in making a transition, and students entering the counseling profession are often in the midst of one or more transitions—from undergraduate to graduate, from student to professional, and sometimes from one profession to another.

Entering graduate school is a difficult time for many students. A study by Valdez (1982) indicated that 89% of the participants in his study experienced a moderate or major crisis during their first semester as graduate students. In addition to the many problems that normally occur with graduate course work, many students struggle with changes in their work situations, finances, living arrangements, and social relationships (R. L. Bowman, Bowman, & Delucia, 1990). Because this is a time of such uncertainty, graduate students are open to and can benefit from mentoring relationships with interested faculty members.

For many counseling students, the initial connection with a mentor occurs through classroom interaction with the faculty member. However, being a mentor requires many more functions than simply being a good or inspiring teacher. In the book *The Seasons of a Man's Life* (Levinson, Darrow, Klein, Levinson, & McKee, 1978), the multiple roles of a mentor are said to include those of teacher, sponsor, guide, exemplar, counselor, and believer. In academic environments, he or she also serves as an evaluator. According to Levinson et al., the mentor's role is a difficult one, because he or she must blend and combine contrasting roles such as counselor–evaluator and guide–believer. It also can be a confusing role for the mentee, because he or she must learn to respond to the mentor in these various roles (Plaut, 1993). For example, often the mentoring relationship might involve the student and the teacher socializing, traveling, and discussing their personal lives. Concurrently, as a mentee, the student might be encouraged to provide honest feedback and opinions to the mentor. However, throughout these various professional and personal activities and interactions, the mentor continues to be the teacher and, therefore, the evaluator. Thus, although the relationship between the mentor and the mentee can indeed be rewarding, it is also often complex and difficult.

The Mentoring Relationship

A mentoring relationship creates a liaison between the student and the teacher that is both personal and professional. Frey and Noller (1983) believe that successful mentoring relationships require a kind of chemistry between the two individuals. According to Kram (1980), it is usually the mentor who initiates this liaison. Most students are unsure of how to ask for mentorship or even if it is appropriate to do so. Being selected as a mentee often feels like an honor to the student, who many times is uncertain about why he or she is being selected. Being chosen provides the student with a sense of validation of his or her potential.

Because being a mentor can require much time and commitment, faculty members are often selective in whom they choose to mentor. In interviews of mentors conducted by Allen, Poteet, and Burroughs (1997), mentors were asked to identify what led them to choose whom they did as mentees. Six "protege attractiveness factors" were described. One was how the protege reflected similar qualities to those of the mentor. A second factor described by the mentors was personality indicators. They explained that they looked for mentees who possessed qualities such as being people-oriented, displaying honesty and integrity, and exuding confidence. A third factor was the mentee's level of motivation, for example, whether he or she displayed a strong work ethic, initiative, or achievement. A fourth factor was competency indicators. Mentors sought out mentees who exhibited indicators of a high capacity or ability. For example, they looked for mentees who were intelligent and who were effective communicators. A fifth factor was whether the mentor believed he or she had something to offer that could be of benefit to the mentee. The final factor was the mentee's learning orientation, his or her willingness to learn and openness to constructive feedback

These findings reflect similar results of other studies. Olian, Carroll, and Giannantonio (1993) found that mentors anticipated greater rewards and were more willing to mentor high-performing students than moderate-performing students. Green and Bauer (1995) found similar results in their 2-year study of entering doctoral students. They discovered that the beginning students who appeared the most capable received the most psychosocial mentoring, career mentoring, and research collaboration.

Of course, mentees also must be open to the mentoring relationship offered by the faculty members who choose them. Mentees must be receptive to the advice and assistance offered by mentors. The most capable and qualified students may be invited into mentoring relationships by several faculty members. Some may choose to have more than one mentor, utilizing the strengths of different faculty members to provide various mentoring needs. Some of the qualities looked for by students in mentors mirror those mentors seek in students. In a study of 71 graduate women, the six characteristics they regarded as most important in their mentors were "willing to share knowledge, honest, competent, willing to let me grow, willing to give positive and critical feedback, and direct in dealing with me" (Knox & McGovern, 1988, p. 40). The choice of a mentor is a significant one. One graduate student stated, "The single most important decision a graduate student can make is his/her major professor. Never faltering faith by the mentor in the mentee can pull us through the graduate maze" (Wilde & Schau, 1991, p. 167).

In mentoring relationships such as these, mentors informally choose students with whom they can identify and with whom they are willing to provide time and attention. The students return the mentors' interest and a relationship is informally created and gradually develops over time. The relationship may never even be identified as a mentoring one. With some, the relationship is so gradual that it is only later that the student realizes he or she has been mentored.

Some counseling programs, however, provide formal mentoring programs in which faculty members and students are placed in mentoring teams through various methods, such as committee assignment, matching based on students' files, or random pairings. Such relationships are "often more superficial than mentoring relationships which have developed informally because chemistry and personal commitment cannot be legislated" (Fagenson-Eland, Marks, & Amendola, 1997, p. 31). Not all formal pairings are successful. The faculty member and the student may feel pressured into the relationship, and one may find the other unworthy of the position that he or she has been given. Assigned mentoring can result in longer adjustment periods and lower levels of commitment by both the mentor and the mentee (Chao, Walz, & Gardner, 1992). Despite these obstacles, mentoring received through formal programs results in more favorable outcomes for those students than for students who receive no mentoring (Chao et al., 1992). These programs may be especially significant and beneficial to those students who might not normally be chosen by mentors as mentees.

It has been shown that the relationships between graduate students and their faculty members are considered by most graduate students as the most important aspect of the quality of their graduate experience (Barger & Mayo-Chamberlain, 1988). Therefore, the majority of students who do not have mentors often have feelings of regret (Swerdlik & Bardon, 1988). There are various reasons why students might not have this experience. Wilde and Schau (1991) found that older students received less professional development in the mentoring they received. They suggested that these students may need and seek fewer of the traditional aspects of mentoring. Some students are too fearful to seek out mentors, whereas others do not see having mentors as an option. Because faculty members often choose the students who have the most potential and who exude confidence and enthusiasm, less confident or assertive students who might benefit from the additional attention may be overlooked. Institutional factors also can influence the lack of mentoring. In university programs in which many of the instructors are part-time, there may be a scarcity of available mentors. Also, in programs in which students commute or attend classes only at night, faculty members and students may not have the necessary time for the relationship to be established and developed. Whatever the cause, students who receive no mentoring often have a less fulfilling graduate experience.

Benefits to the Mentee

Research has indicated that both mentors and mentees benefit from mentoring relationships (Fagenson, 1988; Gerstein, 1985). Through interactions with their mentors on academic, social, professional, and personal levels, the mentees' graduate experience is enhanced. Benefits to the students occur in several areas: interpersonal awareness and development, formation of professional identity, development of professional skills, and professional growth.

The academic and experiential components of a counseling program bring with them the challenges and opportunities for students to increase their personal awareness. Many counseling students experience fear and uncertainty as they begin to learn the skills of their new profession. Often they are challenged through the course work and through the practicum and internship experiences to look within themselves and to become more self-aware. For students who are face-to-face with real-life clients for the first time, many insecurities are likely to surface. Some of these students find encouragement and support from their mentors. L. Duggan (personal communication, September 15, 1998) described what she valued most about her mentor when she felt so unsure of herself:

> I received permission not to know what I was doing. She made it okay to be lost, ignorant, scared, embarrassed—whatever it was I was experiencing. It was okay to be where I was. She "normalized" my feelings and experiences. I didn't have to "fake it." It was okay for my counseling skills to be awful—that didn't reflect on my "self." She acknowledged that I was in a new situation and was inexperienced, but she never treated me like I was inferior. She encouraged me, respected me, and supported me. I felt safe enough to try new techniques, and it wasn't too devastating when I made mistakes.

The safety and security provided by the mentor allowed the student to take risks in her training and to be assured of her own worth. The personal and social interaction between the mentor and the mentee creates a type of intimacy that is not completely professional but also is not completely personal. This allows the student to self-disclose more freely to the mentor, allowing him or her to ask for guidance and assistance. At the same time, as the mentor self-discloses, the mentee is able to see the mentor as a person, and often the mentor's willingness to do this with a student allows the student to see the "person" as well as the "professional." For some mentees, it is this realness that they value and benefit from the most.

The relationship also can benefit the mentee in the formation of his or her professional identity. Many students enter counseling programs unclear about what counselors are and how they are different from other mental health professionals. They do not have a picture of what it means to be a professional counselor. Having a faculty member and mentor who has a clear sense of what it is to be a counselor can assist students in beginning to understand the role and profession they are assuming. This helps them develop a stronger and clearer sense of professional identity. Mentors also can provide such an example of what it means to be a counselor by being role models for mentees. Lee (1998) recalled how when he first met his mentor, the mentor gave him a picture of the type of professional Lee wanted to be:

> I first met Pasteur when I took his class, entitled "Social Systems and Counseling," in the second year of my master's program. He was the first and only African American professor that I had in my training program. I was immediately struck by his presence, knowledge, energy, and the stylish manner in which he dressed. By the end of my first class with Pasteur, I said to myself, "I want to be like him when I grow up!" And it was from that first class with Pasteur that the course of my professional life was set. As my mentor, he has left me with a very rich legacy. (Lee, 1998, p. 8)

Mentors also can be very helpful in the development of their mentees' professional skills (Bova & Phillips, 1984). They often coach their mentees on "the ropes of the profession" (Chao et al., 1992). The mentors teach not only the technical aspects of the profession but also the profession's or department's political workings. They also engage their students in activities and functions that provide exposure and experience for the students (Alleman, Cochran, Doverspike, & Newman, 1984). Mentors can provide guidance on how to become involved in the profession at state and national levels, to become involved in professional organizations, and to be effective leaders in the profession. Mentors can help students move more quickly through their program's requirements and help them define their career goals (Bogat & Redner, 1985). Reskin (1979) found that students with mentors demonstrated higher levels of productivity in research, publication, and presentation of conference papers. Even when mentors are assisting mentees in their professional skills, the interpersonal aspects of the relationship are essential. Betz (1997) suggested that "the mentoring relationship is key to the feelings that students develop about research" (p. 89) and that when conducting research with a mentee, "the crucial ingredient of mentoring is the 'social/interpersonal' aspect of mentoring rather than the actual work experience in the adviser's 'laboratory'" (p. 89).

There can be additional benefits to having had a mentor even after a mentee has left graduate school. Many mentors continue assisting in the professional development of the mentee (Harris & Brewer, 1986). Mentors often help the student make career plans, find his or her first job, and nominate him or her for positions and offices within professional organizations. Graduates and mentors may continue to coauthor publications, write grants, or present together at conferences (Wilde & Schau, 1991). Cameron (1978) also found that faculty mentors improve the student's employment possibilities.

Benefits to the Mentor

Faculty members who were mentored themselves appear to recognize the value in mentoring and are significantly more likely to have mentees themselves (Allen et al., 1997; Busch, 1985). The mentoring relationship, however, is beneficial not only to the student. Busch found that professors recognize that mentoring is important for themselves as well as for their students. In the book *The Mentor Connection*, Zey (1984) suggested that mentoring provides four categories of benefits to mentors: career enhancement, intelligence–information, advisory role, and psychic rewards.

The mentor's career can be enhanced in various ways. Through his or her work with a mentee, the mentor's performance and reputation may be strengthened (Busch, 1985; Hunt & Michael, 1983), and esteem may be gained from peers and superiors (Hunt & Michael, 1983). He or she also may receive organizational recognition and may benefit in improved job performance as a result of receiving a new perspective from his or her mentee (Kram, 1980; Levinson et al., 1978). In addition, professional support can be provided by the mentee in various ways (Busch, 1985).

According to Zey (1984), the mentor's intelligence–information also can be enhanced through work with a mentee. Mullen (1994) suggested that mentoring primarily serves as an information exchange in which mentees are a valuable source of information for their mentors. For example, a student might provide technical skills or assistance that the professor does not possess (Ferriero, 1982). Students are also frequently involved in library research for course work, which can provide professors with the most current studies and information on various subjects. Mentors also report that, at times, they receive a new or fresher point of view on professional organizations or departments through their mentees' perspectives (Kram, 1980).

The mentor also benefits through his or her actions as an adviser. Many professors feel satisfaction in spotting new talent and being in a position to influence and assist novice professionals. In Busch's (1985) study of mentors, the benefit that mentors mentioned most often was being in a position to witness the career and intellectual growth of mentees. Being in the position of adviser also brings a sense of power and gratification (Fagenson, 1988; Gerstein, 1985). Gerstein (1985) found that mentoring provided the mentor with a connection to '"youthful energy in the world and in himself. He needs the recipient of mentoring as much as the recipient needs him" (p. 156). While remaining connected to this youthful energy through offering his or her services, the mentor also is able to feel a connection to the future through serving as an adviser. This may provide a sense of professional immortality:

> The mentor may experience, through the student, the closest one may feel to a professional immortality—a feeling that the baton is being passed to someone worthy and that one's work will live on, not only on the yellowing pages of a journal somewhere in the stacks of a library, but in the mind and work of someone younger, more energetic, and equally committed to the task to which one's professional life has been so fully devoted. (Plaut, 1993, p. 210)

A benefit often mentioned by mentors is the psychic or interpersonal rewards they experience through mentoring. They report experiencing psychological well-being (Ferriero, 1982), self-confirmation (Hunt & Michael, 1983), emotional satisfaction (Kahnweiler & Johnson, 1980), and exhilaration from the energy provided by the ones they mentor (Allen et al., 1997). The relationship also can meet personal needs as mentees provide a source of support (Busch, 1985; Levinson et al., 1978). A relationship that begins as a teacher–student relationship can transform into that of personal friends and valuable colleagues (Busch, 1985; Jacobi, 1991). Faculty members additionally report that their own personal growth occurs as a result of mentoring students (Busch, 1985). Plaut (1993) asserted that the unique mentoring relationship between the faculty member and the student can be a "peak experience" for both the mentor and the mentee and suggested that it is an experience that cannot be found in any other relationship in quite the same way.

Students Mentoring Students

Erwin McCorkle was the doctoral graduate assistant assigned to my practicum class. One day after class, he took me aside and quietly said, "You have a lot of potential." He had watched me struggle from behind the two-way mirror as I stumbled over words and clumsily tried to reflect and restate. I was astounded that he had heard something in my feeble attempts that made him conclude I had promise. But I wanted to believe him, and I trusted that he saw potential in me. So later, when I felt unsure about a research topic, when I was terrified to see my very first real client, when I was questioning whether to go into the doctoral program, I went to him, because he saw something in me and believed in me, and he helped me believe in myself. (C. Woodyard)

The graduate student experience is a difficult one, and perhaps no one can better understand and respond to the problems faced by these students than other students. Both formal and informal mentoring of graduate students occurs by other students who have already navigated some of the difficulties the new students confront. This peer mentoring can be particularly crucial to students who are not chosen as mentees by faculty mentors.

Student mentors provide many types of assistance to fellow students. They often can offer advice on how to avoid the pitfalls of graduate school and can give specific information on classes, faculty, and paperwork. Even if the new student has a faculty mentor, he or she may feel more comfortable asking a student mentor questions that might seem too "dumb" to ask a faculty member (R. L. Bowman et al., 1990). Student mentors can be helpful in furnishing information concerning internship sites, comprehensive exams, and financial aid assistance. Student mentors also provide social support and can assist new students in connecting with other students in the department and organizations within the university. Student mentors also can be great resources for emotional support, because they often best understand what it is their fellow students are facing.

In many departments, doctoral students are used as graduate or teaching assistants. Often, they work with students in prepracticum labs or provide weekly supervision for the master's-level students. They are sometimes in a position to spend more one-on-one time with students than are faculty members. For students without faculty mentors, this relationship may offer their only mentoring experiences. For example, J. Roberts (personal communication, September 10, 1998), a student who was disappointed in not receiving a mentorship from the faculty for whom she had hoped, described the value of what she received from a doctoral-level student who served as a mentor:

> When I went to graduate school, I had great anticipation of being in small classes, of getting to experience the professors' interest in my development, and of receiving some encouragement as I moved through the program. What I experienced was NO interest on any professor's part. That was a real loss for me and fit right in with my old scripts: I'm not valuable, I'm not interesting, I'm not worth spending time on to develop and encourage growth and skills.
>
> Although it wasn't a formal mentoring situation, I experienced my interactions with a doctoral level student as mentoring throughout my graduate experience. From her I experienced positive regard and great encouragement. I felt respect in all of my contacts with her. She was a resource so that I never felt alone or on my own. She provided an underlying support base that helped me to continue to develop and stretch. Although I didn't realize it at the time, she was my mentor all along.

This type of mentoring by one student for another can be invaluable.

Some departments recognize the importance and value of students mentoring other students and provide formal programs in which entering students are matched with an upperclassman who can provide direction and assistance. Valdez (1982) recommended that this pairing of students be done on the basis of the new student's possible needs (e.g., a single mother returning to school, a foreign student) or other common characteristics (both pursuing a school counselor track, live in the same area, etc.). Formal programs are sometimes organized through departmental organizations such as Chi Sigma Iota, an international honor society for counseling students and professionals. Purdue University conducted a program for entering students in their counseling and personnel services department and found that although this type of mentoring was not successful for all students who participated, 100% of those students who met with their mentors three or more times found it positively affected stress associated with the transition to graduate school (R. L. Bowman et al., 1990).

Senior Faculty Mentoring Junior Faculty

My first attempt at counselor education is well underway as of this writing; I am just completing my first year. Thus far, my experience has been characterized by both thrill and agony. Feelings freely associated with my early experiences included loneliness, distraction, guilt, fatigue, and frustration. Equally, however, I had feelings of excitement, confidence, and joy in a dream realized. My story begins with a terrible row with the local energy company, unfriendly neighbors, and an illness in my far-away family. Driving toward my new work environment each morning, I would often have what I have come to term the "Dorothy experience: Toto (or in my case, my faithful cat, Tish), we' re not in ___ anymore." My overwhelming feelings were isolation and confusion. These personal frustrations did riffle to help my early adjustment to academia; nevertheless, I contend that overall, my experiences are fairly normal. (Smith, 1998, p. 11)

The experiences and feelings that Smith described are indeed normal ones for newly graduated PhDs assuming their first positions as faculty members in counselor education departments. This is a very critical period for these novices, and many enter it having left or lost the strong mentoring relationships they experienced as graduate students (Herr, 1994). Once again, mentoring can be of invaluable assistance in making a transition—this time from graduate student to junior faculty member.

Pressures for the New Faculty Member

The transition into the role of faculty member is one that can bring with it many difficult and unpleasant emotions. A cursory reading of the literature on new faculty members finds several words repeatedly used to describe the new faculty members' experiences. They include *tension, alone, isolation, anxiety,* and *worry* (Boice, 1992; Jackson & Simpson, 1994; Sorcinelli, 1988, 1994; Turner & Boice, 1987). In several studies, women and minorities seem especially vulnerable to feelings of isolation and aloneness (Sorcinelli, 1994). At times, the novices enter their new professional role with unrealistic expectations, and they are faced with the conflict between what the job really is and what they had expected it to be (Bova & Phillips, 1984). During the 1st year, many new faculty members complain of physical symptoms such as fatigue, insomnia, and anxiety attacks (Turner & Boice, 1987).

Amidst these uncomfortable and difficult feelings, the new faculty members are often faced with more demands than ever before (Jackson & Simpson, 1994). As new faculty members, they are expected to teach a minimum load, conduct research, and be available for service opportunities to the department and institution. From the beginning, new faculty members are made aware that if they do not meet these requirements, they will not be eligible for tenure and promotion, thus forcing them to leave the institution. Being a good teacher demands much time for planning and preparation. Additionally, there is the challenge of handling difficult students and other problems related to the classroom. Finding time to focus on and devote to research can be particularly burdensome. This can be even more difficult in large research universities, where the pressure to publish is intense. This often results in increased feelings of isolation and aloneness. Jackson and Simpson (1994) asserted that "there is probably no other type of institution where effective mentoring is needed more than in the research university" (pp. 65–66). In addition to these problems, new faculty members often do not have immediate access to or knowledge of the necessary resources and funding to conduct the research they would like to do (Sorcinelli, 1994). Balancing these various commitments and sometimes conflicting roles and responsibilities is no easy task for the new professionals. Turner and Boice (1987) found that 83% of the new faculty members they surveyed described a level of "busyness" that resulted in physical and emotional symptoms.

There are also many questions and unknowns with which new faculty members struggle. Some are practical and specific and are easily answered, for example, the process for obtaining business cards, departmental mailboxes, E-mail addresses, keys, and parking permits. Many questions have to be answered regarding teaching and preparing for class (e.g., availability of and the process by which to obtain audiovisual equipment, xeroxing, book orders, course requirements). Other questions are not related to such immediate concerns and are more difficult to find answers to. For example, new faculty members often have questions regarding how to be successful and satisfy the requirements needed for tenure and promotion (Otto, 1994). They also are faced with understanding the organizational structures, values, history, and traditions of their new department and campus. Getting direct answers to these types of questions is not always easy, because often there are unwritten rules and policies that are informally handed down from generation to generation and are verbally passed along from one colleague to another (Hall & Sandler, 1983). The new faculty members also may have intrapersonal questions with which they have to contend. They may wonder whether they really fit as a counselor educator and a university faculty member. Some also question their own values as they relate to the values of their institutions and disciplines (Kram, 1980).

In addition to these professional challenges, there are also personal pressures with which new faculty members must contend. For faculty members who have just completed graduate school, there can be a rather drastic change in lifestyle and roles. Formerly surrounded by other graduate students facing similar struggles, the new faculty members often feel a lack of collegial relationships. Sorcinelli (1994) found that new faculty report the "lack of collegial relations as the most surprising and disappointing aspect of their first year" (p. 475). Often living in unfamiliar communities, the faculty members must find new social stimulation and support. This can be especially difficult for those who are unmarried and without families. For those with spouses and children, there are additional pressures, however. Finding jobs for spouses, new schools for children, new homes for families, and all of the other tasks that come with moving are demanding. New faculty members often struggle to find a balance between the needs of themselves, their careers, and their families (Sorcinelli, 1994). The accumulation of these pressures can be overwhelming.

The Role of the Senior Faculty Mentor

Departments and universities have recently taken notice of the difficulties facing new and junior faculty mentors. Some have responded to this need by developing formal mentoring programs that pair junior and senior faculty members. Many programs assign the junior faculty member to a senior member in the same department; others pair across departmental lines. In contrast to informal mentoring relationships, these mentorships are more structured and are formally recognized by the department or institution. Programs may require training for the mentor, a commitment for a particular period of time, and periodic meetings between the mentor and the mentee. An example of a formal program is that at Temple University in Philadelphia. Every full-time junior faculty member in the arts and sciences is offered the opportunity to work privately on his or her teaching skills with a senior professor who has recently retired from the university. The pair meets for approximately 90 minutes every 2 weeks during the academic year. Stipends are provided for the mentors, and competitive grants are offered to junior faculty participants (Sorcinelli, 1994).

There are also some models for establishing multiple-mentor programs (Burlew, 1991). Some departments provide several mentors for various functions; for example, a junior faculty member might be assigned three different mentors to assist with his or her teaching, research, and social needs. The University of Georgia provides three different programs for various mentoring needs: the Lilly Teaching Fellows Program, the Institute for Behavioral Research Mentoring Program, and the Teaching Improvement Program (Jackson & Simpson, 1994). Formal mentoring programs such as these are often found to be effective (Sorcinelli, 1994), but Chao et al. (1992) found that compared with informal mentoring, formal mentoring relationships decreased the mentors' motivation and the mentees' openness. They also found that mentees in informal mentorships received slightly more career-related support from their mentors than did mentees in formal mentorships.

In informal mentoring, the junior and senior faculty members choose each other on much the same basis as that of faculty members and graduate students—potential, alikeness, and promise. Many times these informal relationships are based on the existence of a personal chemistry (Frey & Noller, 1983). The new faculty member is likely to seek the assistance of a mentor whom he or she perceives to be successful, powerful, and potentially generative (Otto, 1994). This spontaneous mentoring relationship is more likely to create a deeper level of intimacy and personal connectedness. This type of mentoring might be described as a "'professional intimacy' which involves a professional element with the added element of a close friendship" (Zagumny, 1993, p. 43). At the beginning, one of the greatest challenges for the new pair is for the junior and senior faculty members to create a mentoring relationship rather than a student–teacher relationship (Otto, 1994). This requires the newly graduated student to see himself or herself as a professional and colleague and requires the senior faculty member to see the novice as an inexperienced but valuable colleague with potential.

As in all mentoring relationships, the primary role of the senior faculty mentor is to be a transitional figure for the junior faculty member. When Fink (1992) asked 1st-year faculty for recommendations on how their institutions could have made their 1st year easier and more productive, two thirds said they would have appreciated more specific assistance from fellow faculty members. A mentor can offer support in this transition by providing assistance in many areas.

Senior faculty mentors can provide mentees with some of the practical "nuts-and-bolts" information on the workings of the department and the university. This includes helping them understand the subculture of the department, the college, and the administrative level above the department. It also includes providing them with information on the governing structure and the organizational structure within the university (Herr, 1994). The mentor is needed to help develop the mentee's organizational socialization by providing information concerning the people, politics, history, and goals of the department and the university. The senior faculty member also can be of invaluable assistance in clearly specifying and explaining what will be required for the junior member to achieve tenure and promotion and may even be of help in preparing materials needed for advancement (Fink, 1992; Otto, 1994).

The senior faculty mentor can serve as a source of introduction for the new faculty member. This includes introducing the mentee to key persons on campus and in the community who have access to resources and who are in positions to influence decisions. The mentor also might introduce the mentee to various local and national professional organizations and help the mentee begin to enlarge his or her professional network (Herr, 1994). The senior faculty member also might be instrumental in introducing the mentee to a more clear professional identity as a counselor and counselor educator (Bova & Phillips, 1984).

In addition, new faculty members can benefit from more support and direction in their teaching and research responsibilities. Mentors can provide valuable practical assistance in teaching by sharing assignments, syllabi, books, supplies, and ideas. Offers to team teach or to provide support and advice on dealing with difficult students can be invaluable (Sorcinelli, 1994). Mentors also might monitor the new faculty members' teaching loads, making sure that they are not overly burdened (Herr, 1994). Mentors also can offer to assist in research activities or invite the mentees to join in their ongoing research. This might include joint involvement in grant writing, publication, and presentations. For new faculty members who feel the pressure to publish and who have never done so, this assistance is invaluable. Mentors might provide information on where the new faculty members might locate resources for start-up funds for research projects (Johnsrud, 1994; Otto, 1994).

Mentors also can provide help in the socialization and personal needs of their mentees. They can do this by helping the mentees make connections inside the university and outside in the community. Mentors are the "human connection" that can be vital for the social and intellectual well-being of mentees (Johnsrud, 1994). This might even include helping locate resources needed by the faculty members' partner or children (Herr, 1994). Offering to listen or spending time with mentees away from campus might alleviate some of the mentees' sense of isolation.

Benefits to the Mentee, Mentor, and Institution

Although no specific studies could be found that evaluated the benefits of senior faculty counselor educators mentoring junior faculty, there is research on the overall benefits of mentoring to mentees, mentors, and institutions. Benefits to mentees include growth in their sense of intellectual competence, sense of purpose, feelings of autonomy, and personal integrity (Bova & Phillips, 1984). Mentees are assisted in integrating into the department and institution and are helped in obtaining a sense of belonging (Zey, 1988). Mentees also have been found to have a greater sense of their own power than those who were not mentored (Fagenson, 1988). In addition, mentoring relationships have been found to assist young faculty members in their professional development (Otto, 1994). Having mentors also has been linked to career advancement (Fagenson, 1988, 1989; Scandura, 1992; Whitely, Dougherty, & Dreher, 1992) and to higher pay and greater career satisfaction (Dansky, 1996; Fagenson, 1988, 1989; Olian, Carroll, Giannantonio, & Feren, 1988; Scandura, 1992; Whitely et al., 1992). Rawlins and Rawlins (1983) suggested that "finding a mentor is the most important strategy for climbing the professional ladder" (p. 117).

Gerstein (1985) found that the benefits of the mentoring relationship were indeed reciprocal for both the mentor and the mentee. These included job advancement, more control of the work environment, creation of a support system, increased access to system resources, reputation enhancement, and personal satisfaction. In Allen et al.'s (1997) study of mentoring from the mentors' perspective, they found that mentors listed many benefits to mentoring. Mentors stated that mentoring strengthened their support network through the close relationships they developed with their mentees. They also reported experiencing self-satisfaction through seeing their mentees grow. The mentors found that they benefited in their own jobs through the work with their mentees; for example, mentees helped them complete projects and shared information and knowledge with them. They appreciated the opportunity mentoring provided to ensure the passing on of knowledge to others. Mentoring also has been found to bring recognition to mentors (Otto, 1994).

The institution itself also benefits from the mentoring of junior faculty members. The productivity of both junior and senior faculty members can be enhanced by the mentoring relationship. Compared with those who did not receive mentoring, mentees have been found to be more highly committed to their profession (Wright & Wright, 1987) and to their institutions. This commitment results in junior faculty members being less likely to leave their current positions (Otto, 1994). This is beneficial to the institution because recruiting new faculty members is often costly. Mentees are also likely to provide their organizations with more leadership talent (Fagenson-Eland et al., 1997).

Practitioners Mentoring Practitioners

I don't believe I have been mentored since I was a masters-level student, not as a doctoral student, and certainly not as a professional. I feel that the biggest void in my training is that I never received supervision from a professional who really took the time or had an interest in my work. I have grown into my current professional presence through a lot of self-shaping, not through rigorous supervision. I believe there are pros and cons to that, but few have ever really seen what I do. So, I wonder at times if my work really "cuts the mustard." I have always wanted to be mentored by someone who was strong and ethical and very dedicated to his or her work. I thought that would help me create a solid foundation for my practice. I never got that. Instead, I have been on my own a lot in my professional development. (C. Fox, personal communication, September 23, 1998)

Mentoring seems to occur least between counseling practitioners. Perhaps this is because in its truest sense a mentor is a transitional figure. Once one has become a professional counselor, perhaps he or she is seen to "have arrived," and mentoring is no longer required. Unless it is part of one's job, no longer are there required times for supervision when advice, feedback, and evaluation are provided by a senior-level professional. Instead of mentoring, professionals often turn to colleagues for these services.

A practitioner can serve as a transitional figure for the newly graduated student who is entering the role of professional counselor. Tentoni (1995) suggested that mentoring for these newly emerging professionals can be very beneficial. Such a mentor might assist the new professional in preparing for state licensing exams, setting up a private practice, or understanding the state's political issues related to mental health (Buckner, 1992). Mentors also can be beneficial in helping the new professional establish a professional identity (Good, 1992). Many new practitioners have fears and insecurities about their new role. Gilbert and Rossman (1992) wrote that mentoring professionals can empower and provide sponsorship for such mentees. They can assist young counselors in building a sturdy framework and in knowing how to apply that framework to daily practice. They can provide encouragement and new ideas, skills, and tools. These may include basic information such as how to become an insurance provider, when to refer, when to consult with other professionals, how to talk to physicians, and how to build a professional network. Mentors also might provide up-to-date information on changes in the practice and profession; share current literature in the field; jointly submit proposals for papers, programs, or workshops; allow the mentees to observe them in practice; or provide information on various managed care companies (Tentoni, 1995). This assistance could be invaluable to the transitioning new practitioner.

Many practicing professionals who have made the transition still seek mentorship. Although they are able to turn to colleagues for assistance and feedback, sometimes that does not satisfactorily provide what mentorship might. Also, there is the danger of competitiveness developing between colleagues. Because colleagues are peers, often they cannot provide the supervisory element of mentoring that many practitioners still seek. They may not have the professional maturity or skills that mentors possess to provide beneficial yet critical feedback. Some practitioners receive mentorship through involvement with other practitioners in professional organizations and through leadership opportunities in those organizations. This provides them an avenue to work with more seasoned and experienced professionals and to develop their leadership skills. Still, this is an area of mentorship and professional development for counselors that needs further research, development, and implementation. Encouraging practitioners to continue in supervision when it is no longer required may be one way for practitioners to meet their need for mentoring.

Risks and Challenges of Mentoring

Although there are many benefits to mentoring and being mentored at all levels of the counselor's professional development, the relationship also brings with it many risks and challenges. Inherent in the mentoring relationship is an imbalance of power. The mentor's perceived power by the mentee is one of the initial reasons why the mentor is of interest and value to the mentee. At the same time, this imbalance is one factor that makes the mentoring relationship a difficult one.

This imbalance is particularly sensitive in the mentoring relationship between students and faculty members. Ethical standards clearly state that dual relationships between faculty and students are to be avoided. However, inherent in the mentoring relationship is both an interpersonal and a professional relationship. At times, mentors and mentees may be involved in activities in which they travel together, assist each other on projects, and socialize outside of the university setting. There are no clear guidelines in the area of mentoring on what is allowed in a mentoring relationship and what is stepping out of bounds. In small counselor education programs there may be additional difficulties because the mentor's and the mentee's responsibilities and roles may become more intertwined (V. E. Bowman, Hatley, & Bowman, 1995). For example, a faculty member who is mentoring a doctoral student might be a source of support and encouragement when the student faces personal problems. At the same time, the mentor might be team teaching with the student, directing the student's dissertation, and working with the student as colleagues on a research project. Discerning what is "dual relationship" and what is "appropriate mentoring" can be difficult. However, it is the mentor's responsibility to create and monitor the relationship's boundaries because he or she is in the more powerful position (Plaut, 1993). As the relationship develops and the student begins to behave more as a colleague, which is one of the ultimate goals of mentoring, the more blurred the boundaries become (V. E. Bowman et al., 1995).

The power of mentoring lies in its one-on-one relationship that is focused on the mentee's learning and development. The relationship is often intense, intimate, and personal. Because the boundaries can be so nebulous, some counselor educators develop "dual relationship phobia" (Lloyd, 1992) and avoid mentoring at all. These educators develop rigid boundaries where the roles of "teacher" and "student" are clearly defined. Although this may help them feel more safe and ethical, this can rob the professor, student, and profession of the many benefits that result from the mentoring relationship.

All types of mentoring relationships move through various stages (Otto, 1994), with the ultimate goal of leveling out the power imbalance as the mentor and the mentee become colleagues or friends of similar status (Tentoni, 1995). The process of moving from the beginning stage of the relationship's initiation to the final stage of its redefinition can be a difficult one for both the mentor and the mentee (Otto, 1994).

Levinson et al. (1978) believed that the mentoring relationship is inherently conflictual and creates contradictory emotions within the mentee:

> In a "good enough" mentoring relationship, the young man feels admiration, respect, appreciation, gratitude, and love for the mentor. These outweigh but cannot entirely prevent the opposite feelings: resentment, inferiority, envy, intimidation. There is a resonance between them at different times, or even

at the same moment—he experiences himself as the inept novice, the fraudulent imposter, the equal colleague and the rising star who will someday soar to heights far beyond those of the mentor. (p. 100)

For the graduate student, these ambiguous feelings can be difficult to maintain and manage when they are directed toward an instructor or a dissertation chair. For the junior faculty member, they can create tension and anxiety when having to serve in the same department as the mentoring senior faculty member. Conflicting feelings also can occur within the mentor. For example, he or she cannot help but be pleased and proud of a mentee's success but may feel resentful if the mentee's skill and reputation begin to surpass that of the mentor (Otto, 1994). The interpersonal and professional complexities involved in these relationships can result in many conflicts for both members.

Normal movement through the stages of the mentoring relationship may result in negative feelings within the mentor. For example, in the beginning of the relationship, when the junior faculty member might be most frightened and uncertain, he or she might be overly dependent on the mentor, resulting in the mentor's resentment of the demands on his or her time. Still, at a later time, a power struggle might occur if the junior faculty member disregards the senior faculty mentor's advice and chooses to adhere to his or her own ideas. Also, the mentor might feel discounted if the mentee seeks out the opinions and advice of other faculty members. As the mentee becomes less dependent on the mentor, the mentor might feel abandoned and unappreciated (Otto, 1994).

There are other negatives to both the mentor and the mentee. One of the primary negatives is the time that is required to mentor (Allen et al., 1997; Busch, 1985). If a mentor chooses to mentor more than one mentee, this can become very demanding. Other negatives listed by mentors include perceived favoritism toward the mentee by other faculty members or students, the mentee's abuse of the relationship, and feelings of embarrassment if the mentee fails (Allen et al., 1997). Some mentors also have experienced being backstabbed by those to whom they have devoted so much time and attention. Other faculty members complain that they receive no course credit or compensation for the time they spend with mentees (Busch, 1985).

Mentees also can be hurt in the mentoring process if they are abused or exploited (Green & Bauer, 1995). Because of the power imbalance, they are more vulnerable to being victimized. For example, a graduate student might be used by the mentor to complete tasks outside of a student's regular responsibilities that the student does not want to do. Because of the mentor's position, the student would feel unable to refuse. Kitchner (1992) recommended that before faculty members engage students in such activities, they need to ask themselves how the activity will benefit the students and protect the students' right not to participate. Abuse of power also can occur when the mentor takes primary credit for a publication or a presentation for which the mentee did the majority of the work (Weinrach, 1987). Another negative experience mentees sometimes encounter is jealousy by their peers and claims of favoritism (V. E. Bowman et al., 1995). For the student, this can result in an important loss of support from peers, and for the junior faculty member, this can result in tension between the faculty member and other faculty members, possibly leading to potential political difficulties. Mentors also at times lose sight of their responsibility to help the mentees develop their own individual potential; instead, they create "clones," and the mentees become poor imitators of the mentors' skills and abilities (Zagumny, 1993).

Some of the greatest conflicts in the mentoring relationship occur as the relationship moves toward termination. Because the purpose of a mentorship is to aid in the transition of the mentee, the relationship is, by its very nature, temporary. Ideally, the process can be a gradual and healthy distancing with an eventual reestablishment into a different relationship. However, the mentoring relationship is one in which there are often strong ties and emotional links (Frey & Noller, 1983), and this transition into a new relationship often is not easy.

From the onset, the mentor's role is to foster independence and autonomy in the mentee (Plaut, 1993). Although both the mentor and the mentee may understand that this separation is a necessary developmental phase, to actually go through the process of separation or to begin to assume the stance of equals can be very difficult (Bogart, 1992). This separation of the teacher from the student can happen in various ways and with various outcomes, some more painful to the members than others. Levinson et al. (1978) explained that although some mentoring relationships are able to make the transition relatively smoothly, many do not:

> Most often, however, an intense mentor relationship ends with
> a strong conflict and bad feelings on both sides. The young

man may have powerful feelings of bitterness, rancor, grief, abandonment, liberation, and rejuvenation. The sense of resonance is lost. The mentor, for his part, finds the young man inexplicably tough, unreceptive to even the best counsel, irrationally rebellious and ungrateful. By the time they are through, there is generally some validity in each one's criticism of the other. (pp. 100–101)

Although it is not necessarily so, depending on the situation, both the mentor and the mentee can be left feeling used, discarded, and abandoned or satisfied, proud, and fulfilled.

Conclusion

In conclusion, assuming the role of the mentor or the mentee, whether as a student, a junior or senior faculty member, or a practitioner, involves risk. The relationship can be an incredibly beneficial and rewarding one, but because it requires a blending of both the personal and professional lives of its members, it leaves both the mentor and the mentee vulnerable to disappointment, hurt, and abuse. However, mentorship at all levels can provide invaluable opportunities for professional development and personal enhancement for counselors at all stages of development.

References

Alleman, E., Cochran, J., Doverspike, J., & Newman, I. (1984). Enriching mentoring relationships. *Personnel and Guidance Journal, 62,* 329–332.

Allen, T. D., Poteet, M. L., & Burroughs, S. M. (1997). The mentor's perspective: A qualitative inquiry and future research agenda. *Journal of Vocational Behavior, 51,* 70–89.

Barger, R. R., & Mayo-Chamberlain, J. (1988). Advisor and advisee issues in doctoral education. *Journal of Higher Education, 54,* 407–432.

Betz, N. E. (1997). Increasing research involvement and interests among graduate students in counseling psychology. *The Counseling Psychologist, 25,* 88–93.

Bogart, G. C. (1992). Separating from a spiritual teacher. *Journal of Transpersonal Psychology, 24,* 1–21.

Bogat, G. A., & Redner, R. L. (1985). How mentoring affects the professional development of women in psychology. *Professional Psychology: Research and Practice, 16,* 851–859.

Boice, R. (1992). *The new faculty member.* San Francisco: Jossey-Bass.

Bova, B. M., & Phillips, R. R. (1984). Mentoring as a learning experience for adults. *Journal of Teacher Education, 35,* 16–20.

Bowman, R. L., Bowman, V. E., & Delucia, J. L. (1990). Mentoring in a graduate counseling program: Students helping students. *Counselor Education and Supervision, 30,* 58–65.

Bowman, V. E., Hatley, L. D., & Bowman, R. L. (1995). Faculty–student relationships: The dual role controversy. *Counselor Education and Supervision, 34,* 232–242.

Buckner, M. O. (1992). New professionals in private practice. *The Counseling Psychologist, 20,* 10–16.

Burlew, L. (1991). Multiple mentor model: A conceptual framework. *Journal of Career Development, 17,* 213–221.

Busch, J. W. (1985). Mentoring in graduate schools of education: Mentors' perceptions. *American Educational Research Journal, 22,* 257–265.

Cameron, S. M. (1978, March). *Women in academia: Faculty sponsorship, informal structures, and career success.* Paper presented at the annual meeting of the American Educational Research Association, New York.

Chao, G. T., Walz, P. M., & Gardner, P. D. (1992). Formal and informal mentorships: A comparison on mentoring functions and contrast with nonmentored counterparts. *Personnel Psychology, 45,* 619–636.

Dansky, K. J. (1996). The effect of group mentoring on career outcomes. *Group and Organization Management, 21,* 5–21.

Fagenson, E. A. (1988). The power of a mentor: Proteges' and nonprotege's perceptions of their own power in organizations. *Group and Organization Studies, 13,* 182–194.

Fagenson, E. A. (1989). The mentor advantage: Perceived career/job experiences of proteges versus non-proteges. *Journal of Organizational Behavior, 10,* 309–320.

Fagenson-Eland, E. A., Marks, M. A., & Amendola, K. L. (1997). Perceptions of mentoring relationships. *Journal of Vocational Behavior, 51,* 29–42.

Ferriero, D. S. (1982). ARL directors as proteges and mentors. *Journal of Academic Librarianship, 7,* 358–365.

Fink, L. D. (1992). Orientation programs for new faculty. In M. D. Sorcinelli & A. E. Austin (Eds.), *Developing new and junior faculty* (pp. 141–155). San Francisco: Jossey-Bass.

Frey, B. R., & Noller, R. B. (1983). Mentoring: A legacy of success. *Journal of Creative Behavior, 17,* 60–64.

Gerstein, M. (1985). Mentoring: An age old practice in a knowledge-based society. *Journal of Counseling and Development, 64,* 156–157.

Gilbert, L. A., & Rossman, K. M. (1992). Gender and the mentoring process for women: Implications for professional development. *Professional Psychology: Research and Practice, 23,* 233–238.

Good, G. E. (1992). New and early professionals: Observations and implications. *The Counseling Psychologist, 20,* 82–88.

Green, S. G., & Bauer, T. N. (1995). Supervisory mentoring by advisors: Relationships with doctoral student potential, productivity, and commitment. *Personnel Psychology, 48,* 537–561.

Hall, R. M., & Sandler, B. R. (1983). *Projects on the status and education of women.* Washington, DC: Association of American Congress.

Harris, R. J., & Brewer, C. L. (1986). Mentoring in teaching a university psychology class. In W. A. Gray & M. M. Gray (Eds.), *Mentoring: Aid to excellence in education, the family and the community* (pp. 48–69). Vancouver, British Columbia, Canada: International Association for Mentoring.

Herr, K. U. (1994). Mentoring faculty at the departmental level. In R. J. Menges (Ed.), *Mentoring revisited: Making an impact on individuals and institutions* (pp. 81–90). San Francisco: Jossey-Bass.

Hunt, D. M., & Michael, C. (1983). Mentorship: A career training and development tool. *Academy of Management Review, 8,* 475–485.

Jackson, W. K., & Simpson, R. D. (1994) Mentoring new faculty for teaching and research. In R. J. Menges (Ed.), *Mentoring revisited: Making an impact on individuals and institutions* (pp. 65–72). San Francisco: Jossey-Bass.

Jacobi, M. (1991). Mentoring and undergraduate academic success: A literature review. *Review of Educational Research, 61,* 505–532.

Johnsrud, L. K. (1994). Enabling the success of junior faculty women through mentoring. In R. J. Menges (Ed.), *Mentoring revisited: Making an impact on individuals and institutions* (pp. 53–63). San Francisco: Jossey-Bass.

Kahnweiler, J. B., & Johnson, P. L. (1980). A midlife developmental profile of the returning woman student. *Journal of College Student Personnel, 21,* 414–419.

Kitchner, K. S. (1992). Psychologist as teacher and mentor: Affirming ethical values throughout the curriculum. *Professional Psychology: Research and Practice, 23,* 190–195.

Knox, P. L., & McGovern, T. V. (1988). Mentoring women in academia. *Teaching of Psychology, 15,* 39–41.

Kram, K. E. (1980). *Mentoring processes at work.* Unpublished doctoral dissertation, Yale University.

Lee, C. (1998). Who was your mentor in your leadership development and how did he/she mentor you? *Exemplar, 13*(2), 8.

Levinson, D. J., Darrow, C. M., Klein, E. G., Levinson, M. H., & McKee, B. (1978). *The seasons of a man's life.* New York: Knopf.

Lloyd, A. (1992). Dual relationship problems in counselor education. In B. Herlihy & G. Corey (Eds.), *Dual relationships in counseling* (pp. 59–64). Alexandria, VA: American Association for Counseling and Development.

Mullen, E. (1994). Framing the mentoring relationship as an information exchange. *Human Resource Management Review, 4,* 357–281.

Olian, J. D., Carroll, S. J., & Giannantonio, C. M. (1993). Mentor reactions to proteges: An experiment with managers. *Journal of Vocational Behavior, 43,* 266–278.

Olian, J. D., Carroll, S. J., Giannantonio, C. M., & Feren, D. B. (1988). What do proteges look for in a mentor? Results of three experimental studies. *Journal of Vocational Behavior, 33,* 15–37.

Otto, M. L. (1994). Mentoring: An adult developmental perspective. In R. J. Menges (Ed.), *Mentoring revisited: Making an impact on individuals and institutions* (pp. 15–24). San Francisco: Jossey-Bass.

Plaut, S. M (1993). Boundary issues in teacher–student relationships. *Journal of Sex and Marital Therapy, 19,* 210–219.

Rawlins, M. E., & Rawlins, L. (1983). Mentoring and networking for helping professionals. *Personnel and Guidance Journal, 62,* 116–118.

Reskin, B. F. (1979). Academic sponsorship and scientists' careers. *Sociology of Education, 52,* 129–146.

Scandura, T. A. (1992). Mentorship and career mobility: An empirical investigation. *Journal of Organizational Behavior, 12,* 1–6.

Smith, S. (1998). A "normal" first year counselor educator. *Exemplar, 13*(2), 11–12.

Sorcinelli, M. D. (1988). Satisfaction and concerns of new university teachers. *To Improve the Academy, 7,* 121–133.

Sorcinelli, M. D. (1994). Effective approaches to new faculty development. *Journal of Counseling and Development, 72,* 474–479.

Swerdlik, M. E., & Bardon, J. (1988). A survey of mentoring experiences in school psychology. *Journal of School Psychology, 26,* 213–224.

Tentoni, S. C. (1995). The mentoring of counseling students: A concept in search of a paradigm. *Counselor Education and Supervision, 35,* 32–42.

Turner, J. L., & Boice, R. (1987). Starting at the beginning: Concerns and needs of the new faculty. *To Improve the Academy, 6,* 41–55.

Valdez, R. (1982). First year doctoral students and stress. *College Student Journal, 6,* 30–37.

Weinrach, S. G. (1987). Some serious and some not so serious reactions to AACD and its journals. *Journal of Counseling and Development, 65,* 395–399.

Whitely, W., Dougherty, T. W., & Dreher, G. F. (1992). Correlates of career-oriented mentoring for early career managers and professionals. *Journal of Organizational Behavior, 13,* 141–154.

Wilde, J. B., & Schau, C. G. (1991). Mentoring in graduate school of education: Mentees' perceptions. *Journal of Experimental Education, 59,* 165–179.

Wright, C. A., & Wright, S. D. (1987). The role of mentors in the career development of young professionals. *Family Relations Journal of Applied Family and Child Studies, 36,* 204–208.

Zagumny, M. J. (1993). Mentoring as a tool for change: A social learning perspective. *Organization Development Journal, 11*(4), 43–48.

Zey, M. G. (1984). *The mentor connection.* Homewood, IL: Dow Jones-Irwin.

Zey, M. G. (1988). A mentor for all reasons. *Personnel Journal, 6,* 46–51.

A Marriage (Not) Made in Heaven: School Administrators, Counselors, and Mentoring

By Penny Smith

Remember Viewmasters, those 1950s replacements for the stereoscope? With a satisfying depression of a right side lever, a child could rotate through three-dimensional pictures of exotic places, national parks, or historic monuments. I sometimes picture the introduction of a newly hired educator to a school as a series of those brightly colored images. *Click.* We walk into a new building. *Click.* Passing out staff handbooks and general supplies, a smiling secretary greets us. *Click.* We attend our initial faculty meeting, surrounded by people happily catching up on their summer adventures. *Click.* We walk down a corridor to our place of business.

For a school counselor, however, the pictures then take a different turn. There is an office, not a classroom; a schedule to be set, not a prescribed list of courses and students enrolled therein; a job with multiple, sometimes unseen tasks, not one with a fairly clear public perception of what it entails; and a dearth of fellow counselors, not a number of job-alike colleagues. New counselors, somewhat like new administrators, often find themselves the sole practitioners of that profession in a school. How they behave, what they do, and what their relationships with the other persons in the building are to be become negotiations made from a position of relative isolation. School counselors occupy problematic professional space.

For school counselors, particularly in settings in which there is only one counseling position, several factors complicate these negotiations. There is no peer in the building to facilitate an introduction to their tasks. They are supervised on a daily basis by a practitioner who probably has little or no training in counseling and who has a very different set of professional priorities. If they have a job-alike mentor, he or she is likely to be in another building, removed by distance and time from immediate availability. Additionally, the mentor is likely to be too physically, emotionally, and intellectually removed from the culture of that particular setting to offer place-specific assistance. New counselors are also geographically separated from the universities from which they graduated and unable to readily call on their academic mentors for sustained assistance. Introduction to their school counseling lives is all too often a self-help event. The focus of this chapter is on examining the mentoring process for school counselors and the difficulties that may occur when a school administrator takes on the role of mentor for the school counselor, a frequently occurring event.

Shaping a Professional Identity: Formal Preparation

Bateson (1989), in her felicitously titled book *Composing a Life*, suggests that as we move through time making choices, we become their sum—we compose or shape who we are. We construct our personal lives by weaving together differing portions of biology and experience. We construct our professional lives from role expectations, education, significant others, role models, and experiences mediated by the dynamics of particular settings. We compose ourselves. How we do that is influenced by the people around us and the places we happen to be.

Initially we might have an inclination toward acting out a certain role, a predisposition toward one career or another. Skovholt and Ronnestad (1992) noted that, even before formal professional education begins, a prospective counselor has a commonsense notion of what that role entails and how it should be performed. Untrained, albeit sympathetic toward others, a prospective counselor might seek out or be sought out to play the part of helper. Finding a fit between aspiration and inclination, an individual then enters a period of formal training. Skovholt and Ronnestad argued that there are three professional preparation stages for counselors: transition, imitation, and conditional autonomy. The prospective counselor decides to enter a training program; acquires initial knowledge and skills, which are actualized at a literal or an imitative level; and initiates practice under close supervision in internships. What happens during those three stages corresponds somewhat to the model that Fleming (1953) developed to describe the accumulation of professional skills in psychotherapy training. The prospective counselor learns initially by imitating (do what I say), then by successive approximation of appropriate practice (correct what I critique), and finally by creating (do what works for you within the foundations set for acceptable practice). The counselor's mentor–teacher is first an expert, then a coach, and ultimately a facilitator.

There is a relatively high level of agreement among professional stakeholders about the roles that school counselors should play and about the dimensions of their professional practice. In 1990, the American School Counselor Association (ASCA) identified three processes and five interventions that define the work of school counselors. They counsel, consult, and coordinate by engaging in individual counseling, group counseling, large-group guidance activities, conferencing or staff development, and the management of an array of services. Schmidt (1991) summarized the essential services that school counselors provide as counseling, consulting, and appraising, a division that incorporates in their particulars the tasks outlined by the ASCA. In a later 1996 publication, Schmidt's list included six general services: counseling, consulting, coordinating, appraising, scheduling services, and evaluating results. Myrick (1993) enumerated "six basic counselor interventions," adding "peer facilitation programs and projects" (pp. 83–84) to the ASCA's list. Gysbers and Henderson (2000; see also Gysbers & Moore, 1981) identified four interactive elements of a comprehensive guidance program: guidance curriculum (group guidance), individual planning (advising and assessing), responsive services (counseling, consulting, and referring), and system support (managing, outreach, and public relations). The profession speaks with congruence and clarity about the formal roles that a counselor should play within a school and the components of a well-articulated, comprehensive school guidance program. It does so, however, in a generic sense.

The Importance of Setting

Although the importance of formal preparation for a particular profession is obvious and although part of that preparation is the inculcation of a set of specific professional values, what happens before and after schooling is likewise significant. Professional socialization results from expectations, training, and experience. If that experience takes place within an organization, then it is mediated by that organization's culture. One is socialized professionally as well as organizationally (Bittner, 1965; Manning, 1977).

A profession is distinguished from a job by having certain characteristics. Millerson, in a 1969 study of 20 different definitions of *profession*, concluded that it must possess the following elements:

> (1) application of skills based on technical knowledge; (2) requirements for advanced education and training; (3) some formal testing of competence and control of admission to [the] profession; (4) existence of professional associations; (5) the existence of codes of conducts or ethics; and (6) the existence of an accepted commitment or calling, or sense of responsibility for serving the public. (as quoted in Benveniste, 1987, p. 33)

School counseling, using these criteria, qualifies as a profession.

Hall (1968) approached the criteria for consideration as a profession not from the perspective of specific components of a definition but rather from that of attitudes and values. A profession includes colleagues who have the capacity to generate and judge ideas about practice. Professionals are imbued with a sense of service and a belief that their work provides a public benefit. Like Millerson, Hall thought that professionals respond to a calling. Professionals are autonomous and self-regulating; they place a premium on peer control. Using Hall's criteria, school counseling is less clearly a profession. School counselors work within organizations and under the supervision of noncounselors; their ability to be totally self-directing and autonomous can be and often is limited, sometimes to a considerable extent.

Like teachers and school administrators, school counselors are hybrid professionals. Borrowing from the literature on social workers, we might more appropriately define them as bureau-professionals (Johnson, 1972; May & Buck, 1998; Parry & Parry, 1979). Their identity is influenced by the profession proper; by the state-mediated administrative structures within which they practice; and by a constellation of external pressures that respond to cultural, social, political, and economic changes specific to a particular setting. They function within a duality of professional cultures: one defined by the profession itself (e.g., the ASCA) and one defined by the place in which the profession is practiced.

Prospective school counselors complete a training program that is extensive, rigorous, and shaped by the guidelines established by professional organizations, and they sit for licensure examinations that attest that they possess the requisite knowledge and skills for competent practice. Yet, even then, their role identity as a school counselor is incomplete. They become school counselors through practice within schools. Schools do not exist in cultural vacuums, nor do they exist in some form of idealized virtual reality. They are subject to the vagaries of political decisions, economic declines, and sociodemographic fluctuations. They also are populated by a changing cast of characters, both students and faculty, whose needs and expectations relative to those of school counselors likewise change. Although the ASCA or other professional organizations may prefer to specify the roles that their members will play in such organizations, they can do so only to the degree to which they can influence external policymakers to mandate job descriptions and shape, through education and persuasion, the perceptions that school faculty hold of appropriate counselor roles.

Because individual schools have unique cultures, unique values, and unique expectations, a practitioner's role definition, professional practice, and identity formation will be partially a function of setting. The rules of "how we do things here" are site-dependent and often are invisible to a newcomer. "We think *with* them and do not have to think *about* them" (Langer, 1951, p. 238). Moreover, because school counselors have themselves been to schools where they have observed other counselors through the lens of a student, they sometimes have a preconceived, erroneous notion of what might be helpful in decoding or understanding the school environment. And, because preparation programs often focus on the technical skills of professional activities rather than the social mediation skills necessary to translate them into actual practice, school counselors find that what they were taught to do might not be what they are expected to do.

School counselors are not the only professionals in need of assistance in negotiating the realities of a workplace. Not only are bureau-professionals, by the nature of their work, forced to negotiate professional space and identity, but increasingly, professionals in such fields as law and engineering, because of recent trends from private practice to corporate practice, are having to address autonomy issues (Benveniste, 1987; Myers, 1996; Tansley, 1996). Yet, the knowledge that they are not the only professionals struggling with how to maintain a sense of professional identity within constricting administrative structures, comforting though it may be, fails to address how they should go about the task.

Conflicting Role Expectations

We do not lack succinct, articulate statements about the appropriate roles and functions of school counselors. In 1966, 1981, and 1990, for example, the ASCA provided us with such parameters. Yet, in 1987, the American Counseling Association (ACA), borrowing the language of the Bell Commission, issued *School Counseling: A Profession at Risk,* noting that the future of the profession was in doubt. Six years later, *The Crisis in School Counseling* (ACA, 1993) indicated that the profession was under siege by its critics. Harrison (1993) concluded that "the scope of practice for counselors . . . has essentially been by default" (p. 326). As an earlier commentator observed, "Counselors have contributed to their own extinction by not fighting to spend their time doing what they are uniquely trained to do" (Drury, 1984, p. 235). For all the clarity of the ASCA's and the ACA's statements on professional practice, there remains at least the perception of a disparity among what the profession recommends, what other educational stakeholders perceive to be appropriate roles and functions, and what counselors actually do in a specific setting. Because school counselors work in schools, their roles and functions are determined partially by expectations held by others in those organizations.

Investigation of the ways in which various constituencies define what a counselor should do or how a guidance program should function has been a popular area of scholarly inquiry for decades. A 1973 study of Alaskan guidance programs by Spanziani, for instance, demonstrated that administrators and counselors defined the responsibilities of the latter differently. Spanziani et al. called for a clarification of counselors' obligations. Conversely, reflective of increasing agreement among stakeholders, Miller's 1989 study of elementary school counselors, teachers, and parents found congruence among these constituencies on the importance of guidance programs and the appropriate activities of counselors. Findings on role perceptions differ by time and place. They also differ somewhat by level (elementary, middle, or high school) and function (roles played by the respondents in the various studies).

Perceptual differences were more likely to occur in the early days of comprehensive guidance programs and appear to have lessened as we approach the end of the century. Assisted by the National Defense Education Act of 1958, which financed training to increase the number of available counselors, secondary school guidance can be said to have come of age in the 1960s. However, there was not agreement about what counselors should do nor about whether they should be perceived as members of the teaching faculty or as members of the administrative staff (Gibson, 1990; Gibson & Mitchell, 1986). Ellis (1972) found that there were differences among counselors, administrators, and counselor educators about perceived and actual roles. Boyd (1973) noted that counselors were assigned tasks, often administrative in nature, that were unrelated to their guidance responsibilities. Hart and Price (1970) described differences between principals and counselor educators about school counselors' roles.

Valine, Higgins, and Hatcher (1982) surveyed teachers in two southeastern communities in 1972 and 1980, asking them about their perceptions of counselors' roles. Noting that "teacher expectations of counselors and teacher knowledge of counselor performance can have great impact upon students, parents, and administrators" (p. 211), Valine et al. found that both confusion about roles and mixed opinions about counselor effectiveness existed. Although teachers were more positive in 1980 about having counselors in schools than they were in 1972, they were more likely to see them as ineffective. When they were asked whether they understood the role of the school counselor, 62% in 1972 answered either "no" or "undecided" to that survey item. Although that figure dropped to 49% in 1980, it was probably disturbing to counselors that nearly half of their school colleagues did not know what they did.

Gibson (1990) compared the opinions of teachers about high school guidance programs in 1965 and in 1986. He, too, concluded that counselors had failed "to adequately communicate" (p. 254) what they were about. Only 28% of the faculty that responded to the 1965 survey were uncertain that they could tell a new student about available guidance services in their school. Yet that figure did not improve substantially by 1986, when 27% of the respondents answered either "no" or "not sure" to the same survey item. Whereas 84% of the 1965 respondents believed that the guidance program had a positive impact on the school's instructional program, only 72% felt that was true in 1986. Whereas 98% of the faculties in 1965 believed that teachers would confer with counselors about student problems, only 71% replied in the affirmative two decades later. These differences notwithstanding, there was relative agreement on what the responsibilities of school counselors should be and that agreement corresponded well with what the professional organizations set as proper roles and functions. The only responsibility of the 10 listed on the survey that changed rank number by more than two places over the 21 years was related to assisting with college placement, a reflection of the increasing number of students seeking postsecondary education more than a disagreement of substance. Counseling students individually remained the top priority for teachers in both surveys; group guidance, consultation about career development, and interpretation of standardized assessments were ranked in the top half of the list. Both surveys found that administrative duties unrelated to the guidance program were the lowest priority of the 10 items.

A lack of clarity about roles and the hesitancy of some teachers to use counselors in areas in which they are trained persist in the 1990s, although several of the congruence themes that Gibson (1990) found have become even more apparent in the present decade. For example, McDowell (1995), in a survey of administrators, counselors, and teachers, found no significant differences in their perceptions of counselor roles related to counseling functions per se. There were differences among teachers with regard to certain administrative functions, such as scheduling.

Peaslee (1991) surveyed administrators, counselors, teachers, and parents about the roles and functions of elementary school counselors. She found that congruence among stakeholders was likely to occur in large school districts and in schools that were served by a counselor. Positive views of counselors were found more often in districts with mature guidance programs than in those without programs (Snyder & Daly, 1993). O'Dell, Rak, Chermonte, Hamlin, and Waina (1996) concluded that disagreements about the efficacy of guidance programs can be divided into four categories: role confusion, delivery of services, public misconceptions, and leadership. Programs that were well staffed, well led, and met students' needs were recognized as important contributors to the overall effectiveness of the schools in which they operated.

When there is congruence among constituents about how one should enact a particular role, performances are valued and clear. When that congruence disappears, through ignorance or experience with less than able practitioners of particular roles, contending perceptions make it difficult to determine what a role should be. O'Dell et al. (1996) found that in guidance programs that were not functioning well, a primary cause was that "nobody could agree on the role of the counselor. Counselors were either suffering from work overload or their skills were being under-used" (p. 305). Roles that are defined differently by professions and particular organizations become dysfunctional. If roles are played, then, within organizations, there are important reasons to facilitate greater congruence between how those roles are defined by the profession and by the organizations in which they are practiced.

Induction and Professional Identity

The literature on induction and mentoring of new educators is extensive and has increased as a result of a heightened emphasis on attracting and retaining quality practitioners. For example, the National Commission on Teaching and America's Future (1996) stressed the importance of comprehensive, quality mentoring programs that link senior practitioners with individuals starting their professional careers:

> Research shows that beginning teachers who have had the continuous support of a skilled mentor are much more likely to stay in the profession and much more likely to get beyond classroom management concerns to focus on student learning. . . . Ideally the first year or two teaching should be structured much like a residency in medicine, with teachers continually consulting a seasoned veteran in their teaching field about the decisions they are making and receiving ongoing advice and evaluation. (pp. 80–81)

Many state policymakers, in response to those recommendations or in anticipation of them, have established comprehensive mentoring programs for new teachers. The National Commission on Teaching and America's Future highlights the work of Connecticut and Toledo, Ohio. However, it just as easily could have referenced work in other states and cities.

The National Foundation for the Improvement of Education (NFIE) likewise stressed the importance of mentoring in its 1996 report titled *Teachers Take Charge of Their Own Learning: Transforming Professional Development for Student Success*. The NFIE noted that "a sustained, school-based, teacher-to-teacher induction process . . . is of vital importance to the continuity of program and sustainability of shared philosophy" (p. 40). It decried the assumption that teaching within a particular organization requires only generic skills and knowledge. Furthermore, the NFIE noted that the introduction to a place is so important that even experienced teachers should be assigned mentors and the appropriate location for induction activities is a specific site and not the system.

In education we have for too long, as the National Commission on Teaching and America's Future (1996) reminded us, relied on a "sink or swim" mentality. We assumed that, by themselves, new teachers were able to translate what they had learned in preservice programs into immediate, sustained, effective practice. Although we know what facilitates the transition from formal training to independent practice, we have rarely provided the resources, in terms of time, personnel, and money, toward such efforts. As recently as 1996, the NFIE found that only 17% of teachers participated in a formal induction program and that 52% participated in no induction program at all (p. 41).

What has been true for teachers is likewise true for school counselors, most of whom are classified as teachers in state statutes and thereby are subject to the rights, responsibilities, and procedural requirements of those practitioners. However, teachers expect to find other teachers in schools, educators whose daily professional lives resemble their own. They are supervised by administrators who have, in most instances, been teachers themselves and are personally familiar with the challenges of that role. That is generally not the case for counselors. If, as Bowman and Stott (1994) argued, how we make sense of our professional world is a social process that involves the interaction of self and culture, then the absence or limited applicability of existing formal induction programs will have a potentially negative effect on practice. Newcomers will be operating without the benefit of social cues; newcomers who do not find role models present in the same building will have fewer cues on which to base professional behavior than will those fortunate enough to have job-alike colleagues working with them.

136

Skovholt and Ronnestad (1992), in their study of counselors' professional development, suggested that conditional autonomy, the final stage of preservice preparation, leads to the initial stage of independent practice or exploration. In conditional autonomy, a counselor participates in a full-time internship under university supervision. In exploration, a counselor has a degree or a certificate and, potentially, a professional license to practice. He or she exits the control of counselor educators, emancipated from the constraints of formal preparation, and enters practice.

Two phases characterize the stage of entering practice: confirmation and disillusionment. Initially, the counselor confirms the accuracy or helpfulness of what was learned in preservice and internship activities by putting those ideas and skills to work in actual practice. The counselor engages in the process of validating formal training programs. However, practice precipitates disillusionment as one realizes that there are numbers of contingencies for which there is neither a ready nor a completely effective response. The professional counselor experiences a sense of disappointment that he or she has not been adequately prepared to address every counseling encounter with equal confidence. He or she struggles to build a personal framework on which to base or structure practice. That professional work, though, is done without the benefit and supervision of "professional elders." "The freedom is often welcomed and feels wonderful. But it also leads to another much more surprising response at times—the loneliness and uncertainty of suddenly being in command of one's own work" (Skovholt & Ronnestad, 1992, p. 53).

In response, the newly liberated counselor seeks, as sources of influence, workplace mentors. Peers, colleagues, and clients become influential in shaping the counselor's sense of professional self. Because school counselors are supervised by and regularly interact with building administrators, they potentially constitute one of the most powerful sources of influence during the induction period of a counselor's career.

Administrators and Counselors

The relationship between administrators and school counselors has long been the subject of scholarly inquiry and anecdotal examination. As Myrick (1993) reminded us, during the immediate post-Sputnik era, many counselors, products of hastily planned preparation programs, found themselves custodians of poorly conceived guidance programs. As a consequence, they "drifted into quasi-administrative positions" (Myrick, 1993, p. 7). Since that time, the profession has been attempting to recast its image from administrator surrogates, master schedule-makers, clerks overseeing college admissions applications, or test coordinators to one that is more consonant with counseling functions.

Emerging from that period with an administrator-independent professional counselor identity has not been easy. For example, early studies indicated tension between counselors and administrators (Herr & Cramer, 1965). Administrators sometimes acknowledged that they preferred counselors whose roles emphasized student achievement and dissemination of information rather than counseling (Knowles & Shertzer, 1965). That lack of early role definition contributed to a tendency to have counselors perform tasks not consistent with those for which their training prepared them (Peters, 1962). Boyd (1973) surveyed 110 principals and counselors and found that there was evidence of conflict between the two groups in reporting what each did, the degree of autonomous power assumed by counselors, and the assignment of noncounseling duties. Hart and Price (1970) found that principals and counselor educators disagreed significantly on some counselor roles, including clerical duties, confidentiality, noncounseling tasks, and certain types of counseling proper.

A continuing dilemma regarding the counselor–principal relationship involves the direct supervision and evaluation of personnel and programs in the guidance area. Principals are occasionally accused of having little knowledge or understanding of what counselors actually or should do. Lampe's (1985) study of 376 schools that provided graduate-level training for both educational administrators and counselors found that the former received insufficient information about the roles and functions of the latter. Some counselors appear to have agreed with those findings, asserting that their administrators did not appreciate what they did (Moracco, Butcke, & McEwan, 1984). Even in 1996, Schmidt wrote about the "inconsistent perceptions by administrators and teachers [that] add to the confusion about the school counselor's role" (p. 23).

Independent of studies that explore other aspects of what has the potential to be a troubling professional relationship, two things appear obvious. First, the principal is a significant determiner of the roles a counselor plays in the school organization (Baker, 1992; Salmon, 1985). Second, there are reasons for potential conflict because of the dramatically different ways that school administrators and school counselors view schools (Cole, 1991).

Kaplan (1995) argued that both real and potential conflicts are derived from the fact that school administrators and counselors see their professional worlds through very different eyes. Administrators focus on the big picture, on the entire school community; counselors generally concentrate on parts of that community and often only on individual students. Administrators are charged with enhancing student learning, currently a responsibility measured by standardized test results on narrow areas of academic competency. Conversely, counselors are more concerned with helping a person grow in a variety of ways that are not always readily measurable or reflective of an emphasis on prescribed academic achievement. Administrators manage resources, both human and material. Counselors facilitate and help; their role is to provide assistance. Administrators solve problems, whereas counselors work to enable other people to identify and solve problems. Administrators measure their success in part by the educational health of an entire community; counselors focus on the mental health of individuals as well as the creation of a healthy mental climate for the school community. They use, in the words of Kaplan, "different paradigms" (p. 261).

Additionally, there are several specific issues on which administrators and counselors will disagree because of their differing worldviews. For example, principals want to know what is happening and what is likely to happen in their schools. They desire information and are likely to look askance at individuals who fail to provide data that might prove helpful in operating a school. Counselors, conversely, must abide by a rule of confidentiality to maintain the trust of their clients. The need to maintain confidentiality automatically conceals certain information from principals. Principals worry about the safety and order of their schools and, consequently, see student discipline issues as problems that threaten such orderliness. Counselors view discipline incidents as opportunities for individual growth, for identifying issues and choices, and for nurturing better problem-solving skills among young people. Administrators often advocate for students as a collective and, necessarily, sometimes sacrifice individual causes for the well-being of the group. Counselors work with students rather than with the student body.

Recent studies have suggested that there is growing congruence, however, among administrators and counselors on how the latter should function. Bonebrake and Borgers (1984) surveyed 184 principals and 212 counselors on the role of secondary school guidance personnel and found that their perceptions were quite similar. Partin (1990) surveyed 710 counselors and 207 principals in Ohio and found that there was general agreement on the ideal and actual ways that counselors spent their time. Those findings were confirmed by Stickel (1990), who used the Counselor Role Inventory in 105 western schools to ascertain constituency role perceptions. Although he identified congruent patterns on only 11 of the 35 possible points of agreement, divergent patterns were small. Yet, anecdotal evidence of divisions persists. Patterson, for example, when asked about changing perceptions of school counseling replied that

> one of the problems is that so many administrators don't understand counseling, don't accept it, don't recognize it as a profession. They expect counselors to do the jobs that they don't have the time to do or don't want to do—discipline, record keeping, that sort of thing. (as quoted in Poidevant, 1991, p. 92)

Additionally, there is evidence that in situations in which there is an additional counselor, the importance of the principal in influencing role formation is lessened. Brott (1997), in a recent study on professional identity formation, found that interactions with administrators, while important, were less significant than interactions with other groups. Of the various publics with which a counselor engages in a school organization, Brott found co-counselors had particularly powerful influences on identity formation. Because her study was done in an urban area in which mature counseling programs existed, its applicability to school settings with immature programs, programs in transition, or programs without other counselors is unclear.

So, although evidence exists that actual disparity between administrators and counselors on professional roles is diminishing, perceived disparity persists in some quarters. Although evidence exists that the role of the principal in shaping counselor practice is less dominant than it once might have been, it remains an important factor, if only because the principal usually retains the power to evaluate counselor performance, to allocate resources, to assign and schedule school personnel, and to define objectives for specific programs. There is, then, a need to consider formal induction programs that facilitate a transition from preservice training to actual practice in ways that are consistent with what we know about effective and appropriate professional counselor conduct in school settings.

Mentoring and Professional Identity

What do experienced counselors need to know about new settings? What do new counselors need to know? In answering these questions, standard introductory texts in the field of school counseling assume the importance of the principal–counselor relationship. Gysbers and Henderson (in press) noted that new counselors need to become familiar with the current guidance program, the school site, the culture of the organization, and the priorities of the principal. Schmidt (1996), acknowledging the supervisory role of building administrators, urged continuous engagement with administrators.

> [It is] essential for principals and counselors to collaborate about the design of the counseling program, selection of major goals and objectives, identification of essential functions, evaluation of services, and countless other details related to comprehensive school counseling programs. This collaboration between principals and counselors is an ongoing process that enables counselors to include their principals in program planning processes and, at the same time, to inform school administrators of issues affecting students' educational development. (p. 177)

Counselors "are the eyes and ears of the school community, helping the principal stay in tune with the needs of students, parents, and teachers" (Schmidt, 1991, p. 195).

How one should collaborate and toward what ends one should work collaboratively are functions of role perception. Role definitions, as argued above, are mediated by others and are place-specific. Matthes (1992), in a study of 40 novice counselors, found that they often work in isolation with little support or direct supervision. They sink or swim essentially alone. They become professionally only what they can negotiate individually. To move away from a reliance on informal or minimal formal induction directed by a non-counselor supervisor, several counselor educators have advocated specific, formal induction programs involving experienced mentors.

Patterson (1989) noted that although there is a growing literature on mentoring new educational professionals, there is considerably less information available on working with new counselors. Local districts often are forced to design programs independently. Matthes (1992) documented new counselors' needs, including ways to resolve role confusion and isolation, and affirmed the hegemonic position held by administrators in determining counselors' roles

141

within schools. Other studies have confirmed the absence of sustained professional assistance during the induction period (see, e.g., Borders & Usher, 1992). An obvious response to such conditions is conscious, formal induction facilitated by experienced counselor practitioners.

VanZandt and Perry (1992) described a statewide mentoring program in Maine that provided new counselors with assistance during their 1st year on the job. They helped establish a formal mechanism to address transition challenges. To support the process, they cited the natural disillusionment that novice counselors encounter, their relative isolation in Maine schools, their supervision by individuals with limited training in counseling, and the hesitancy of counselors to provide advice to their new colleagues as reasons to consider a comprehensive, formal induction program. Their program had four parts: (a) selecting and training mentors, (b) developing and delivering mentor training, (c) pairing mentors and novices for the purpose of professional support, and (d) evaluating results of the mentorship on professional practice.

Mentor training centered on awareness of self as mentors, career development of professional counselors, and appropriate mentor roles. Thirty-six experienced counselors were trained, and in the fall of 1989, 23 of them were matched with 28 novice counselors scattered throughout the state. Mentor–novice pairs then interacted independently throughout the academic year. They were given wide latitude for defining the ways in which they would function. Six months into the academic year, participants evaluated the program, and their responses helped develop the program parameters to be used with a second cohort of counseling novices the following year.

Actual contacts between mentors and novices proved to be infrequent. In the first 6 months, personal contacts averaged fewer than 3, whereas telephone contacts averaged between 3.7 and 5.1 conversations, depending on whether data were reported by mentors or 1st-year counselors. However, both groups indicated that they valued the support provided; they also judged the program to be very worthwhile. The major drawback, according to both groups, was the geographic distance between some participants, a factor that probably contributed to the infrequency of personal contact reported by some pairs.

Drawing on these experiences, VanZandt and Perry (1992) listed seven recommendations for practitioners considering the establishment of a statewide mentoring program. They included (a) promoting mentoring as professionally enhancing; (b) avoiding the exclusive use of self-selection in determining mentors; (c) being geographically inclusive and site-sensitive; (d) designing a sophisticated training package for mentor preparation, one that recognized that mentors were experienced and able practitioners who already possessed mature facilitation skills; (e) recognizing participation through some system of rewards and acknowledgment; (f) finding venues that permit mentor–mentee networking beyond the original pairings; and (g) including visualization as a training tool.

Peace (1995) created a different training model for North Carolina to prepare experienced practitioners to work as mentors to new counselors. Adapting the training design used in that state to prepare teacher mentors, Peace crafted the Counselor Mentor Education Program to enhance the developmental growth of both experienced counselors and, through them, novices. Professional development occurred as a result of role playing, guided reflection, independent practice, support, cognitive dissonance, and continuity. Mentors were asked to (a) establish a professional relationship with a novice counselor; (b) model appropriate, effective counseling skills; (c) engage in a cycle of clinical supervision with their novice counselor; (d) assess the developmental readiness and professional needs of their mentee; and (e) design and provide assistance for that individual. Peace found that there was documented growth in counselor skills among participants and improved supervisory skills among the experienced counselors. Because of the developmental nature of the model Peace used, she claimed that it was applicable for both experienced and novice counselors as well as counseling interns. She concluded that "perhaps a concerted focus on the induction phase will result in our profession . . . increasing its efforts to maximize the potential of both novice and experienced counselors' development" (Peace, 1995, p. 187).

Paisley and Benshoff (1996) noted that we have generally relied on counselors assuming responsibility for their professional development after they exit preparation programs. Yet, we know that the skills and knowledge that are necessary for highly effective, mature practice come over time; they are developmental in nature. In the same way that we compose our personal lives over time and in reaction to encounters with other people, we construct our professional lives in response to practice and results as well as critical reflection on what we did and what happened as a result. To do that well, we need support, challenging feedback, and the consultation of our colleagues.

As a noncounselor and a former school principal who was placed in the position of having supervisory responsibilities for a system's guidance programs in Grades Preschool through 12 when I became an associate superintendent, I asked our counselors ($N = 9$) to help me to identify their professional development needs. We did so through a series of focus groups that I facilitated. What emerged from those sessions were two explicit and unanimous recommendations for professional growth: (a) formal opportunities to talk together about their programs in ways that did not compromise confidentiality but that encouraged supportive questioning and (b) an ongoing opportunity to engage in conversations with experts about their professional practice. Given that we had several novice or relatively new-to-practice counselors in our group as well as experienced practitioners, it was interesting that both sets identified a need for a supportive network of job-alike peers. Both novice and experienced counselors complained of a sense of isolation and identified the need to talk with job-alike colleagues about troubling issues of practice. Novices were particularly interested in what their programs should entail within the general expectations of the system and how those programs articulated what happened at other school levels or across schools within levels.

Regardless of profession, arguably our best induction tool is dialogue, and our best professional growth tool is critical inquiry with colleagues. However, many educational practitioners work in relative isolation, deprived of an opportunity for dialogue as well as opportunities for observing the professional practice of others. Induction programs that include mentoring mitigate those conditions. Even in the absence of an extensive, formal induction program, simply establishing conditions that permit regular conversations among job-alike practitioners has beneficial effects for both novice and veteran counselors. It creates an opportunity for group mentorship, albeit of an informal nature. However, clinical supervision models now being developed for teachers in various locations nationwide hold the promise for making such opportunities for group mentorship formal and more common (see, e.g., NFIE, 1996, pp. 20–37).

Toward a Sustained Congruence of Expectations

We assume that the continued presence of school counselors is an important part of educational organizations in the future. We know the appropriate roles and functions that such individuals should play and that the actual performance of such roles and functions is mediated by place. How, then, can we make it likely that what counselors have been trained and ought to do is what they actually do in school settings? The more consistent the agreement is between representatives of the profession of school counseling and educational stakeholders in schools, the more likely that what a counselor should do and what a counselor does do are the same. Additionally, the more counselor-wise the personnel involved in formal or informal induction activities, the more likely that appropriate professional identity development of novice counselors is facilitated. These assumptions have implications for preservice programs, induction activities, and career development.

Rarely does preservice preparation of school counselors occur in settings where there are not preservice preparation programs for school administrators. Yet, somewhat reminiscent of Snow's famous 1959/1965 essay on the separation between the arts and the sciences, there appears to be a chasm that divides these two regions of inquiry. However, in most school settings, representatives from these two disciplines work side by side, sometimes closer than any other two people in a building. In schools in which the degree of collaboration, trust, and interaction results in a partnership, there appears to be a high congruence of role expectations for counselors and of program objectives for guidance departments (Cooper & Sheffield, 1994; Huey, 1987; Vaught, 1995). Without formal interaction among representatives of these two groups during the preservice training of each, then whatever collaboration results in the field is a result of individual initiatives. One place, then, to begin to ensure some congruence about expectations is before counselors and administrators work together in schools; we need to begin during their professional preparation programs.

Two ways for this process to occur are obvious: In isolation, each discipline can talk about what one needs to know of the other, or in tandem, there can be opportunities for the two disciplines to learn together. Given the potential for separate agendas and mixed messages to occur in the former, although that is the way such matters are generally conducted today, the latter course appears to be the road to travel. School practitioners meet occasionally in courses identified as being part of a professional core common to all educators. That might be a place for a dialogue on mutual expectations to occur. Or, there might be courses designed specifically for school personnel from different areas to explore issues of collaboration and teamwork. Or, there might be a conscious effort to use interdisciplinary courses on skills that are essential for success in both arenas as a way to ensure that Kaplan's (1995) two paradigms can be made to intersect. Whatever institutional resolution is tried, perpetuating separation and isolation or encouraging the continuation of professional core intermingling that fails to address such issues seems an inadequate response.

Another preservice issue for which a resolution might assist in the establishment of a bridge between the worlds of administrators and counselors involves a reintroduction of the importance of place in practice. Preservice programs for both counselors and administrators rarely attach importance to conscious explorations of place, or if they do, they usually attend to the multicultural aspects of urban settings. Yet, professional isolation is most likely to occur in rural settings, rarely a topic of place-specific sensitivity training. All bureau-professionals negotiate identity in organizations. In addition to the knowledge and skills associated with a profession, they need knowledge and skills about negotiating roles within specific social settings. Our preparation programs are context-neutral in ways that do not facilitate the transition from controlled environments and supervised internships to isolated sites of autonomous professional practice.

There is little argument that formal induction and mentoring programs facilitate a smooth transition from preservice training to practice. Yet, the Maine experiment with a statewide induction program revealed the limitations that geography can impose on the desire for close, sustained contact with a role model (VanZandt & Perry, 1992). To overcome the limitations of geography and the likelihood that the daily mentor will be a noncounselor, local schools or school systems sometimes pair novice counselors with experienced practitioners elsewhere in the system. Assignment of a counselor mentor outside the school works only insofar as there are opportunities for the two to meet and discuss induction issues. Time is a resource that must be part of any induction program; it is almost as important as personnel.

School administrators can and should function as knowledgeable guides to the culture of particular settings or can assign experienced teachers to those roles. However, they must realize the need for a professional guide as well and must, in the absence of such guidance, facilitate ways to secure those opportunities for novice counselors. Although face-to-face mentoring is ideal, electronic media provide us with ways to minimize the effects of distance. Asynchronous mentoring, given the power and immediacy of the Internet and E-mail, is an alternative worth exploring. Assuming we can find ways to eliminate the confidentiality issues that might come into play in an electronic conversation among colleagues, computers provide an inexpensive method for traversing distance and also provide multiple means for discussions among several participants. Computers provide unique options for seeing and hearing one or more colleagues while staying at one's desk in an isolated school site. Additionally, computers and interactive distance teleconferencing can provide opportunities for professional development through conversations with experts as well as support for the disillusioned, isolated novice through networks of job-alike colleagues.

Finally, induction is not the end of one's career development. Mentors are desirable, but insufficient, messengers for continued growth, which generally relies on the wisdom of multiple practitioners. As we in education increasingly recognize the need to facilitate career development as a crucial factor in retaining experienced, proficient practitioners, we will cease to consider minimizing the negative effects of isolated practice as exclusively being a novice need. Peace (1995) found that serving as mentors enhanced the professional development of the mentors themselves. Colleges and universities have long recognized the need to provide space and time for scholars to interact, to discuss, to debate, and to test theoretical constructs or practical experiments. The recent emphasis on professional growth of teachers may stimulate consideration of the professional growth of all educators and precipitate a recognition that some school jobs are done without the benefit of daily contact with similar professions. Such consideration should then lead to finding ways to bridge distances within schools among practitioners of different specialties and among schools for practitioners with similar responsibilities. The resultant conversations might help to eliminate discordant perceptions among practitioners and contradictory expectations of them.

Conclusion

Professional identity is forged from preservice training and practice. In fields such as school counseling, in which autonomy is circumscribed by organizational constraints and culture, professional identity is dependent on an organization's values and expectations.

These are often mediated through an administrator who neither knows counseling nor is willing to concede full autonomy to a counseling program. Consequently, professional identity is made more difficult by potentially competing perceptions of competent practice. What the profession per se says sometimes contradicts what a site administrator and staff expect at a particular school.

Evidence exists that induction programs and mentors are helpful in shaping professional identity for educational practitioners, although the evidence for counselors remains less robust than that for teachers because there are few such programs in existence. Yet, what evidence does exist supports the proposition that novice counselors benefit from formal induction programs that include opportunities to work with or be mentored by experienced school counselors. Because an on-site mentor is not always possible for every novice counselor and because daily supervision by an on-site noncounselor administrator is likely, the profession needs to explore ways in which mentor program alternatives can operate and administrators and counselors can know more about each other's work.

References

American Counseling Association. (1987). *School counseling: A profession at risk*. Alexandria, VA: American Counseling Association.

American Counseling Association. (1993). *The crisis in school counseling*. Alexandria, VA: American Counseling Association Press.

American School Counselor Association. (1990). *Role statement: The school counselor*. Alexandria, VA: American Counseling Association Press.

Baker, S. B. (1992). *School counseling for the twenty-first century*. New York: Macmillan.

Bateson, M. C. (1989). *Composing a life*. New York: Atlantic Monthly Press.

Benveniste, G. (1987). *Professionalizing the organization: Reducing bureaucracy to enhance effectiveness*. San Francisco: Jossey-Bass.

Bittner, E. (1965). The concept of organizations. *Social Research, 32,* 239–255.

Bonebrake, C. R., & Borgers, S. B. (1984, February). Counselor roles as perceived by counselors and principals. *Elementary School Guidance and Counseling, 18,* 194–199.

Borders, L. D., & Usher, C. H. (1992). Post-degree supervision: Existing and preferred practice. *Journal of Counseling and Development, 70,* 594–599.

Bowman, B. T., & Stott, F. M. (1994). Understanding development in a cultural context: The challenge for teachers. In B. Malloy & R. New (Eds.),

Diversity and developmentally appropriate practice (pp. 119–134). New York: Teachers College Press.

Boyd, G. A. (1973). *To determine some criteria for defining the role-depiction of the counselor as perceived by the administrator and the role of the administrator as perceived by the counselor in order to further facilitate student development at the secondary level* (ERIC Document Reproduction Service No. ED 096 585).

Brott, P. E. (1997). The development of school counselor identity (Doctoral dissertation, University of North Carolina at Greensboro, 1996). *Dissertation Abstracts International, 57,* 5059–5315.

Cole, C. (1991). Counselor and administrator: A comparison of roles. *NASSP Bulletin, 75,* 5–13.

Cooper, D. E., & Sheffield, S. B. (1994). The principal–counselor relationship in a quality high school. In D. G. Burgess & R. M. Dedmond (Eds.), *Quality leadership and the professional school counselor* (pp. 101–113). Alexandria, VA: American Counseling Association.

Drury, S. S. (1984). Counselor survival in the 1980s. *The School Counselor, 31,* 234–240.

Ellis, F. E. (1972). *The dichotomy between the actual and the perceived role of the elementary guidance counselor in the state of Massachusetts* (ERIC Document Reproduction Service No. ED 068 868).

Fleming, J. (1953). The role of supervision in psychiatric training. *Bulletin of the Menninger Clinic, 17,* 157–159.

Gibson, R. L. (1990). Teachers' opinions of high school counseling and guidance programs: Then and now. *The School Counselor, 37,* 248–255.

Gibson, R. L., & Mitchell, M. H. (1986). *Introduction to counseling and guidance* (2nd ed.). New York: Macmillan.

Gysbers, N. C., & Henderson, P. (2000). *Developing and managing your school guidance program* (3rd ed.). Alexandria, VA: American Counseling Association.

Gysbers, N. C., & Moore, E. J. (1981). *Improving guidance programs.* Englewood Cliffs, NJ: Prentice Hall.

Hall, R. H. (1968). Professionalization and bureaucratization. *American Sociological Review, 33,* 92–104.

Harrison, T. C. (1993). School counseling: Establishing a professional definition. *The Clearing House, 66,* 325–326.

Hart, D. H., & Price, D. J. (1970). Role conflict for school counselors: Training versus job demands. *Personnel Guidance, 48,* 374–379.

Herr, E. L., & Cramer, S. H. (1965). Counselor role determinants as perceived by counselor educators and school counselors. *Counselor Education and Supervision, 5,* 3–20.

Huey, W. C. (1987). The principal–counselor partnership: A winning combination. *NASSP Bulletin, 71*(499), 14–16, 18.

Johnson, T. J. (1972). *Professions and power.* New York: Macmillan.

Kaplan, L. S. (1995). Principals versus counselors: Resolving tension from different practice models. *The School Counselor, 42,* 261–267.

Knowles, R. R., & Shertzer, B. (1965). Attitudes toward the school counselor's role. *Counselor Education and Supervision, 5,* 9–20.

Lampe, R. E. (1985). Principals training in counseling and development: A national survey. *Counselor Education and Supervision, 25,* 44–47.

Langer, S. (1951). *Philosophy in a new key* (2nd ed.). New York: New American Library.

Manning, P. (1977). Talking and becoming: A view of organizational socialization. In R. L. Blankenship (Ed.), *Colleagues in organizations: The social construction of professional work* (pp. 181–201). New York: Wiley.

Matthes, W. A. (1992). Induction of counselors to the profession. *The School Counselor, 39,* 245–250.

May, T., & Buck, M. (1998). Power, professionalism, and organisational transformation. *Sociological Research Online, 3*(2). (http://www.socresonline.org.uk/socresonline/3/2/5.html)

McDowell, D. K. (1995). *Role perception of school counselors* (ERIC Reproduction Services No. ED 3888 909).

Miller, G. D. (1989). What roles and functions do elementary school counselors have? *Elementary School Guidance and Counseling, 24,* 77–88.

Moracco, J. C., Butcke, P. G., & McEwan, M. K. (1984). Measuring stress in school counselors: Some research findings and implications. *The School Counselor, 32,* 110–118.

Myers, E. W. (1996). "Simple truths" about moral education. *American University Law Review, 45*(3). (http://www.wcl.american.edu/pub/journals/lawrev/MYERS.HTM.1)

Myrick, R. D. (1993). *Developmental guidance and counseling: A practical approach* (2nd ed.). Minneapolis, MN: Educational Media Corporation.

National Commission on Teaching and America's Future. (1996). *What matters most: Teaching for America's future.* New York: Author.

National Foundation for the Improvement of Education. (1996). *Teachers take charge of their own learning: Transforming professional development for student success.* Washington, DC: Author.

O'Dell, F. L., Rak, C. F., Chermonte, J. P., Hamlin, A., & Waina, N. (1996). Guidance in the 1990s: Revitalizing the counselor's role. *The Clearing House, 69,* 303–307.

Paisley, P. O., & Benshoff, J. M. (1996). Applying developmental principles to practice: Training issues for the professional development of school counselors. *Elementary School Guidance and Counseling, 30,* 163–169.

Parry, N., & Parry, J. (1979). Social work, professionalism and the state. In N. Parry, M. Rustin, & C. Satyamurti (Eds.), *Social work, welfare and the state* (pp. 21–47). London: Edward Arnold.

Partin, R. L. (1990). *School counselors' time: A comparison of counselors' and principals' perceptions and desires* (ERIC Reproduction Services No. ED 316 786).

Patterson, R. H. (1989). A counselor mentoring program: A mentor's perspective. *The School Counselor, 36,* 167–172.

Peace, S. D. (1995). *A study of school counselor induction: A cognitive–developmental mentor/supervisor training program.* Unpublished doctoral dissertation, North Carolina State University, Raleigh.

Peaslee, M. K. (1991). *The importance of roles and functions of elementary school counselors as perceived by administrators, counselors, teachers, and parents* (ERIC Reproduction Services No. ED 339 953).

Peters, D. (1962). *The status of guidance and counseling in the nation's schools.* Washington, DC: American Counseling Association.

Poidevant, J. M. (1991). Perspectives on school counseling—C. H. Patterson: A personal view. *Elementary School Guidance and Counseling, 26,* 83–95.

Salmon, V. R. (1985) Pupil services. In J. S. Kaiser (Ed.), *The principalship* (pp. 179–212). Minneapolis, MN: Burgess.

Schmidt, J. J. (1991). *A survival guide for the elementary/middle school counselor.* West Nyack, NY: Center for Applied Research in Education.

Schmidt, J. J. (1996). *Counseling in schools: Essential services and comprehensive programs* (2nd ed.). Boston: Allyn & Bacon.

Skovholt, T. M., & Ronnestad, M. H. (1992). *The evolving professional self: Stages and themes in therapist and counselor development.* New York: Wiley.

Snow, C. P. (1965). *The two cultures.* Cambridge, England: Cambridge University Press. (Original work published 1959)

Snyder, B., & Daly, T. (1993). Restructuring guidance and counseloring programs. *The School Counselor, 41,* 36–43.

Spanziani, R. L. (1973). *An evaluation of secondary school guidance and counseling programs in Alaska, Phase 1* (ERIC Reproduction Services No. ED 092 840).

Stickel, S. A. (1990). *A study of role congruence between school counselors and principals* (ERIC Reproduction Services No. ED 321 944).

Tansley, G. D. (1996). Super-Curricular Content: The dissemination of professional culture. *Australian Journal of Engineering, 7*(1). (http://elecpress.monash.edu.au/ajec/vol7no1/tansley.htm)

Valine, W. J., Higgins, E. B., & Hatcher, R. B. (1982). Teacher attitudes toward the role of counselor: An eight-year follow-up study. *The School Counselor, 29,* 208–211.

VanZandt, C. E., & Perry, N. S. (1992) Helping the rookie counselor: A mentoring project. *The School Counselor, 39,* 158–163.

Vaught, C. C. (1995). A letter from a middle school counselor to her principal. *NASSP Bulletin, 70*(570), 20–23.

10

Passing It On: Mentoring Stories

By Mary D. Deck

*I*nvolvement in a mentoring relationship is an intensely inter-personal experience requiring not only an investment of time and effort but also the expenditure of considerable emotional energy and commitment. Developing an ongoing mentoring relationship that changes over time is one of the most complicated professional interactions in which we can engage. Ideally, mentoring relationships are entered into voluntarily, develop over time in ways that benefit the mentor and the protégé, and end in a timely manner, based on a mutual acceptance of changing needs and roles. At the time of termination, the mentor and the protégé are prepared to redefine and reestablish a different professional and personal connection. In reality, mentoring relationships take on a life of their own. These complex human relationships have their own distinctive beginnings. They develop their unique interpersonal histories through the emergence and interplay of multiple professional and personal influences. Through mentoring, a dynamic human story is created; the relationship shifts, changes, and ends in order to take a changed form. Each person is affected for better or worse by the connection.

All of us have stories of how we have been changed by our mentoring experiences. Our involvement with others as mentors and protégés is marked by particular incidents and events that altered the nature of our mentoring relationships and affected our perspectives of ourselves and our work as counselors. In negotiating the intimacies and intricacies of mentoring, we become different persons and professionals. Over the past two decades in the counseling profession, mentoring stories have come my way. As I recall such stories, I invite you to reflect on your experiences. I expect that you will be able to identify similar or related stories that underscore the power of the mentoring process in your own professional development and work. The stories identify some of the issues that significantly impact the degree to which mentoring can create connected, empowered relationships. The stories center on considerations when one is initiating mentoring relationships, power and political influences in mentoring, the usefulness of having multiple mentors within a focused time frame, the need for changing mentors over time, the role conflicts inherent in mentoring, and difficulties in ending and redefining the mentoring relationship.

I Wonder If You Want a Mentoring Relationship: Initiation Stories

When Valerie L. Schwiebert accepted a position as a counselor educator in the program in which I was an associate professor and from which I had graduated as a master's student, I assumed that I would become her mentor. Arrogant, yes. Naive, yes. That was a critical lesson for me about mentoring, unquestionably. My assumption was based to some extent on the fact that I am older than she is by more than 10 years and on my then 15-year history with the program. Less conscious and more hidden needs influencing my assumption were my desire to move more directly into the role of professional elder and to be viewed as a "senior faculty" member by a junior faculty member. This motivation was perhaps prompted by the shift and changes I recently had experienced with my own mentors: the retirement of one, the prolonged illness of another, and changes in rank and association when another was promoted within the university.

During the summer before Valerie arrived, I was talking with a friend and colleague from the university's counseling center about changes in the counseling program and Valerie's joining the faculty. I expressed that I expected to be Valerie's mentor. My friend looked at me quizzically, and in her most gentle, challenging tone responded, "I wonder if she wants you to be her mentor." In that moment, I was struck by the awareness that I had given no thought to whether Valerie would want or need a mentoring relationship with me. I began to reflect on my friend's challenge: "I wonder if she wants you to be her mentor." Valerie was coming with exceptional credentials, and although she had completed her PhD more recently than I had (a factor of our age difference), she had extensive experience in her field and already had accumulated 4 years of faculty experience in a tenure-track position at a major university. Maybe she did not want or need me as a mentor. By accepting the challenge, I realized I needed to wait and allow my professional relationship with Valerie to unfold and not enter into it with my own agenda, expectations, and roles.

Several years later, another situation occurred that caused me to reflect again on the question of being a mentor in a somewhat different context. After about the 3rd day of the fall semester, I was sitting in my office, when one of the young, new faculty members in the college appeared at my door. She was fresh from a doctoral program, youthful in appearance, and full of the exuberance and energy of one just beginning her career as a college professor. With a bright, open smile, she introduced herself and named an administrator who had instructed her to come see me and to ask me to be her mentor. I was caught off-guard and was very flustered. I already was having a hard start to the academic year, experiencing some frustrations and disillusionments that come with years in the bureaucracy of higher education. It was not the time for me to be initiating a novice faculty member into the academy. I was too provoked by, and reactive to, the system to help someone enter it. When she came to me and announced that she had been directed to me, I was dismayed. I embarrassed her and myself with my shocked look and my quick and short response. She experienced the anger I felt toward the administrator who had failed to ask me, "I wonder if you want to be a mentor this year."

These stories indicate that we, counselors, need to examine our reasons and our readiness for becoming mentors. With Valerie, I had not fully explored some of the deeper reasons for wanting to be her mentor, my need to assume the professional elder role. When the new faculty member came to me, I was clearly not at a point emotionally to be able to invest in a mentoring relationship. As counselors, we need to engage in the preliminary self-searching that precedes any other interpersonal work: counseling, supervising, and consulting. We must be willing first to look inward. We need to consider our history, life experiences, beliefs, needs, values, and desires as we undertake participation in a mentoring relationship. Our assumptions, biases, stereotypes, unexplored needs, and hopes can lead to frustration, disappointment, and harm if we are not open to self-examination. Without self-awareness, in our mentoring of others, as when we counsel others, we may enter relationships and unintentionally focus on our purposes, goals, and needs rather than those of our protégés or clients.

We must assess our psychological and situational readiness for mentoring as well. The semester that the new faculty member approached me, I was not psychologically prepared to offer her a meaningful or empowering relationship. Another example of a counselor's readiness to mentor became painfully clear to me a few years ago. A supervisor who assumes a mentoring role with our interns experienced a tragic family loss. He was scheduled to have an intern but called our program and asked us to place the student elsewhere. He knew that he was not ready to take on the intense interpersonal connection that would be required. In time, the supervisor called and said he was again ready to work as a mentor with an intern. Such self-knowledge and self-care are essential for counselors to be effective mentors and parallel counselors' openness to recognizing the level of psychological preparation needed for counseling clients.

Helping others explore their reasons for seeking a mentor and their readiness for working with a mentor is also a crucial aspect when initiating mentoring relationships. A school counselor recently shared a story with me. She had talked with a child about the possibility of working with a Big Sister. The child agreed this might be a good idea. The counselor began to make the necessary contacts. A few days later, the student returned to the counselor and asked, "Will you be mad if I tell you something?" The counselor sensed that the child wanted to talk about the Big Sister idea. Being invited to share, the student acknowledged that she did not really want a Big Sister at that time. We need to be open to the possibility that others may not want or need mentoring relationships, as the school counselor learned from the student, and as I learned from being challenged with the question, "I wonder if she wants you to be her mentor."

Will the Real Mentor Please Stand Up?
A Tale of Power and Politics

Counseling students often select their programs of study because a specific person is on the faculty. They may know of a person's reputation as a researcher or an author and desire to study, learn, and be mentored by the professional they have esteemed. What happens when this desire meets reality and the expectation goes awry? Such is the nature of the following personal account that an acquaintance shared:

At first, I did not realize how my advisor was isolating me from other faculty and students. I trusted her. She was nationally known, and I, in fact, had chosen that doctoral program in counselor ed. hoping to be mentored by her . . . so, I was flattered that she had requested me as an advisee and was taking me under her tutorage. In my first semester, she advised me to take classes I had little interest in taking, including a small three person seminar with her (failing to inform me about a seminar in which the other entering doctoral students were enrolled). She said she was helping me prepare to choose a doctoral committee, and I believed she was acting in good faith and was being the mentor I had wanted.

Before long, her influence seemed to exceed my doctoral program—she was giving me unsolicited advice in personal areas of my life: family matters, finances, social gatherings, even the upkeep of my car! She told me I was wasting my money when I shared that I had invited other graduate students to my house for a meal. I was seeing more and more clearly that she was not the mentor I had imagined she would be. I was not feeling mentored but overpowered by her intrusions into my social and personal life.

Even her feedback on my academic work seemed to be growing more subjective and felt like a power struggle rather than an educational experience. . . I remember the Wednesday before Thanksgiving, she refused to accept my seminar paper, ordering me to have a complete rewrite in her office the following Monday by 9:00 a.m. Intended or not, she seemed to want to control my time. I ended up canceling my Thanksgiving travel plans to stay in town and type all week-end (remember, these were pre-personal computer days . . . no cut and paste!).

Fortunately, she had advised me to enroll in a course with the chair of the program whom I liked and respected . . . but, it appeared my advisor had a lot of clout in the program, so I did not consider going to the chair about my advisor's treatment of me. I felt stuck and did not know how to change things, and I

157

had begun to consider leaving the program at the end of the academic year as my only escape from my mentor.

The final blow came the day I met with her to register for spring courses. She directed me toward courses again that were not in my areas of interest and that would prevent me from taking the graduate instructor assignment I had been offered. When I expressed my desire to teach, she laughed and said I was a student and needed to act like one. Fearful it might mean I would be forced to leave the program at the end of the semester, I again told her that teaching was an important part of my being in the doctoral program. She became angry and ordered me out of her office. In tears, I walked by the office of the program chair. Seeing me in tears, she called me in and without asking me what was wrong, quietly said, "You need to know that this is your doctoral program. It is not any one else's. If you need to talk, feel free to come see me." I slowly walked home in the December chill thinking that maybe I had someone on my side more powerful than my advisor was . . . I felt I had a real mentor for the first time. I had the first good night's sleep I had known in weeks.

The next morning, I went directly to the program chair's office. We talked for over an hour, and I trusted she would support me . . . not only support me but would prevent any retaliation toward me if changes were made. Leaving the chair's office, I went to my advisor's office and requested another advisor effective that day. She tried to dissuade me but I could not be convinced. When I walked out of her office that day, I never entered it again. The program chair honored her commitment to me, reassigned me, and if there were after-effects, I never knew it. My doctoral program became mine . . . soon I was involved in a number of projects in my areas of interest. I was encouraged and supported . . . and I finished my degree on time.

As this story sadly shows, trust, knowledge, and presumed goodwill from a mentor who is a counseling professional may not hold true. The protégé's vulnerability and the mentor's abuse of power, betrayal of trust, and exploitation of perceived expertise are painful themes and are even more alarming when the mentor's profession is counseling. Protégés, working with mentors in the counseling profession, may be even more susceptible to a mentor's abuse of power and roles. Having a counseling professional as a mentor, protégés may be affected by the social influence the counseling title infers (Egan, 1998). Protégés may enter into mentoring relationships with the presumption that counseling mentors will be trustworthy, share expertise, and act benevolently toward them. Counselors and counselor educators who mentor must recognize the inferential power of their positions; work to deserve the trust, respect, and prestige that is conferred on them; and exercise care that their behavior with protégés is ethical and professional.

The story also underscores the value of the protégé establishing a mentoring relationship based on mutual trust and positive regard with someone who exerts influence and commands respect inside the political system of the organization. The student in this story entered the system relying on her mentor to help guide and direct her, only to experience the mentor sabotaging her. Expecting her mentor to respond to her needs as a naive, entering doctoral student, the student soon recognized that her mentoring needs were being ignored and undermined as the mentor set goals and plans that did not meet the student's needs or desires, but rather those of the mentor. The student felt powerless, unaware, and uncertain about how to challenge her mentor's authority. Perhaps the student felt scared, intimidated, and even suspicious of the political system that apparently had given her adviser so much freedom. Feeling powerless, the student was prepared to sacrifice her program, the only option she saw. Only when the student felt supported by the program chair, whose power and influence exceeded those of the adviser, was the student able to enter the system and access its benefits. Mentors need to assert their authority within the system and advocate for protégés to ensure that the political system works to empower and advance the development of protégés. Mentors who assert their power over the lives of the protégés are robbing their protégés of empowerment and self-determination, just as such abuse of power by counselors would rob clients of their rights to choose for themselves.

At times, protégés are not aware of how they are caught in a system and need to be educated about political realities. A colleague tells the story of being vocal and indiscriminate in his criticisms of college policies and procedures when he was a master's-level counseling student. He had been self-employed in another field for 10 years and was unaccustomed to the hierarchy of university politics and how his opinions were being received. Two junior professors called him in and helped him understand how his views were contributing to senior faculty's and administrators' perceptions that he was resistant, arrogant, and insubordinate. He needed assistance in recognizing how he was jeopardizing his future in the program. Mentors also have a responsibility to help protégés understand that organizations have implicit and explicit power structures and that often it is those with inferential powers who are central to building effective networks and to securing opportunities and services. For example, in teaching school counseling students, I remind them that positive interactions with school secretaries are often central to their gaining support in the school, that school librarians are their first source for securing additional resources, and that at times the school custodian knows better than anyone else how to connect with and help a student who is struggling. Counselors who serve as mentors need to understand and help protégés understand power and politics in organizations in order for protégés to flourish in the system.

How Many Mentors Can You Name?
All Around, Mentors Watching Over Me . . .

Reflect back, how many mentors have you had in your professional development? One day I sat down and listed all the people who had served as some type of mentor in my life. I stopped when my list numbered 50 plus, and afterwards, I realized I had omitted my grandmother's name, so it certainly remains an incomplete list. Not all of the people I listed acted as official mentors nor were they counseling professionals. Many were. When I was named a high school counselor with no experience and limited training, a colleague in a nearby high school became my first counseling mentor. She invited me to her school, shared creative and progressive ideas, and was the person I called regularly when I needed information and support. She is now the director of counseling in that school system.

Other early mentors included the male professors in my master's school counseling program (in the late 1970s, all the professors in that counseling program were men; a woman did not join their ranks until 1989). They gave me my initiation into the possibilities of being a counselor educator. One coauthored my first professional publication, another invited me to teach and supervise with him, and the third included me as a presenter at my first regional and national professional conferences. The support and encouragement these men offered and the opportunities they made available when I was a master's student empowered me to consider becoming a counselor educator. Their ongoing professional connections with me over the ensuing years prompted me to reunite with them as a faculty colleague in 1990.

During my doctoral program, there were mentors all around. Looking back, I was fortunate to be surrounded by so many mentors at different professional levels. I met my primary mentor when I approached her, asking if I could observe her teaching a master's introductory counseling skills class for the entire semester. I knew that being an understudy and observer was one of my preferred learning styles. She cautiously looked at me, saying that no one had ever made such a request and she needed to consider it. She told me to check with her in a day or so. That was her first teaching lesson, the first of many. In the 3 years I worked with her, I never knew her not to wait and reflect on a request, an invaluable lesson that I still have not mastered. She chaired my dissertation committee, invited me to teach with her on campus and off, and involved me in professional development projects. Other senior faculty functioned in mentoring roles as encouragers, sponsors, and models of varying styles of professional leadership.

Junior faculty members also served as mentors. More subtle than senior faculty, perhaps because of their own untenured status and our similarity in ages, their mentoring was no less critical in my professional development. One was my supervisor for 2 years, and he was the person I called at 6:00 a.m. during my first semester as a new PhD. I wanted his reassurance that I was competent before I taught my first doctoral-level seminar in supervision. The other junior faculty member became my confidant and my friend. She helped me work through the writing blocks that were preventing me from starting my dissertation and later celebrated with me by taking me to lunch on the day of my dissertation defense.

Fellow doctoral students were peer mentors. Those ahead of me offered advice, shared resources, and gave comfort that the seemingly unending process was manageable and could be completed. Those progressing with me were confidants and sources of laughter and humor amidst the anxious and tense schedule of deadlines, papers, exams, classes, and internships. I remember with gratitude my colleague who sat outside the door during my dissertation defense, supporting me with his presence.

Another mentor who cannot go overlooked during this time was my first personal counselor. I had survived childhood loss and pain; from my family I had learned to forge on in life regardless of the grief and deep sadness I felt over my mother's death when she was only 36. However, in the early weeks of my doctoral program, I was filled with loneliness, anxiety, fear, and confusion that I could not contain. I also was approaching my mother's age when she died, and I was feeling very vulnerable. Feeling so much emotion and pain, I entered counseling. There, I found another mentor. My counselor opened herself to my story, my tears, my anger, my doubts, and my grief, to feelings and experiences I had hidden for so long. She sat with me as I mourned and grieved the pain of being a motherless daughter. She took me into her care, mentoring me as her client in very nurturing and supportive ways. For instance, when I had a surgical procedure, she called me in the hospital to check on me, understanding my panic and fear as I wondered if I, too, would face an early death. She helped me learn to be a "good client," such as challenging my need to control when she turned the clock away from me to prevent me from shutting down as the session was ending. She empowered me to trust the counseling process, to trust a counselor with my story and my pain, and to connect more deeply and more honestly with myself than I ever had.

Looking back at the various mentors I have known at differing stages of my professional development supports Burlew's (1992) contention that multiple mentors are needed across a person's career. As we progress and move in our careers, we need a series of different mentoring relationships to respond to changes in our careers and life stages. My experiences of having differing mentoring relationships as I negotiated specific stages in my career and life were also invaluable to me. To have three very different mentors as a master's student and as a doctoral student to have mentors at each professional level provided me with an array of diverse mentors. Each empowered me, connecting and mentoring me in a unique way.

When counselors act as mentors, we need to help protégés explore other potential mentoring relationships as well. This requires us to be open and generous in acknowledging that a protégé may need several different types of mentoring relationships within a distinct time period, as well as across time. Although I have gained from having multiple mentoring relationships in my life, I realize I can be selfish and petty about sharing my protégés with others. A personal experience brought this lesson of my needing to be more open and generous vividly home to me. My protégé in this instance was my nephew, Samuel, then 5 years old. We were gathered for a family reunion, and I was eager to spend special time with Samuel. We had been great buddies since his birth. During the weekend reunion, I grew increasingly jealous of how much attention and time Samuel was giving my younger brother. As the weekend came to a close, I pulled Samuel aside asking, "Has Aunt Mary lost her buddy?" With all the wisdom and boundless openness of a child, he hugged me and said, "I can have more than one buddy." What a profound lesson he taught me!

In my mentoring of students, I am sometimes in that same place. I feel jealous when others mentor "my" protégé, or I am resistant to hearing about new mentors that graduates acquire when they leave our program. However, I try to remember Samuel's teaching and recall the value of the many mentors who have touched my life. We need to encourage our protégés to have as many mentors as they can watching over them and empowering them. With a variety of mentors, the protégé has exposure to persons with diverse styles and viewpoints and can draw from a wealth of mixed influences and strengths. Having strong connections with a number of mentors and multiple mentoring experiences also may offset some of the potentially negative outcomes that can result when mentors and protégés experience conflicts in their relationships.

What's Happening? I Thought You Were on My Side: The Inevitable Role Conflicts

A counselor serving as a mentor assumes any number of roles when working with a protégé: advocate, supporter, confidant, friend, sponsor, coach, visionary, model, protector, counselor, adviser, expert, initiator, diplomat, networker, teacher, politician, trainer, supervisor, facilitator, colleague, challenger, and evaluator. The shifting of responsibilities and boundaries between mentoring roles can create a number of potential conflicts and contribute to confusion, tension, disappointment, and possible disruption in the mentoring relationship.

This story came to me from a new counselor in the field. He was being mentored by an older, experienced male counselor in a community mental health center. Changes occurred in the administrative structure of the center. The experienced counselor was reassigned to be the novice counselor's supervisor, responsible for evaluating his work during the probationary employment period. During their first supervision session, they discussed the changes in roles. The younger counselor indicated that he thought it would not affect him to have his supervisor also continue as his mentor. Over the next few weeks, however, the mentor recognized that the younger counselor was becoming more distant and reluctant to share with the mentor outside of the supervision time. When the mentor questioned the counselor about his increasing disengagement, the counselor acknowledged being less willing to take personal risks, seek out the mentor for advice and direction, and act spontaneously since he had assumed an evaluative role. At that point, the pair decided to end the mentoring relationship for the present time, and the experienced counselor helped link the new counselor with another mentor in the agency.

In this story, the mentor made efforts to clarify roles and address the protégé's anxiety after changes in their roles occurred. The mentor took the lead in acknowledging changes in the relationship, was open to examining the protégé's reluctance to continue as a protégé, and supported the protégé by helping him establish another mentoring relationship. This story ends more positively than some such stories might.

In many mentoring relationships, the evaluative component of the mentor's role is inescapable. For example, counseling students seek mentors among the faculty, and faculty typically want to mentor students in master's and doctoral programs. Faculty are also continuously monitoring students' progress during their training as part of the faculty's ethical responsibility to oversee the welfare of clients and to be gatekeepers of the profession. In other academic cases, junior faculty are mentored by senior faculty, who also evaluate the junior faculty in their efforts for tenure and promotion. In employment settings, a mentor could be chosen who has no evaluative role over the protégé. Practically, for employees in small agencies or institutions, the mentor may not be able to avoid evaluative roles.

It is the obligation of the mentor to initiate conversations with the protégé about possible role conflicts. This is especially critical when very sensitive and crucial issues such as evaluation are part of the mentor's responsibility to the institution. Counseling protégés often are caught off-guard if such conversations do not happen. They can enter into situations with their mentors expecting unconditional support, and when they experience their mentors in their more challenging, confrontational, or evaluative roles, the protégés can feel confused and bewildered, or worse, betrayed and exploited. Counselors have ethical responsibilities to avoid dual relationships with clients and, if unavoidable, to discuss with clients the implications, limitations, and constraints that dual roles create in the counseling relationship. Similarly, it is the mentor's responsibility to discuss from the onset the possible risks and conflicts that can result in the varying roles that can occur in the mentoring relationship and to establish healthy boundaries for the mentoring connection.

Not all mentoring role conflicts are as obvious or as potentially contentious as the evaluator role can be. Yet, role conflicts are virtually unavoidable in mentoring relationships. The mentor and the protégé have a responsibility to examine the inner struggles that role conflicts precipitate. These struggles can be important signals that the protégé is growing away from the mentor and that a change in the relationship is under way. When I was a junior faculty member, my mentor, a senior faculty member and chair of the program, involved me in a number of professional projects. She offered me nationwide networking opportunities. Her vision about the degree to which I needed to be involved nationally and her role as my confidant and friend collided when she requested on a Monday that I attend a meeting in Washington, DC, on that Friday. The meeting would extend through the following Monday. I had very mixed emotions—flattered that she asked, exhausted from already having been out of town for three consecutive weekends on professional business, and very overwhelmed trying to find some degree of balance between my professional and my personal life. I felt the vice grip of wanting to please her and accept yet another incredible professional opportunity; however, I desperately needed time at home and time to catch up. It was hard to go to her and talk about my conflicting feelings. As much as she was a visionary, she was moreover my supporter, my confidant, and my friend. I trusted she would listen, and although she might be disappointed, she would accept my decision not to attend the meeting, which is what she did.

Until It's Time for You to Go:
Separating and Redefining Who We Are

I consider the story above to be one of the transitional events in moving away from my mentor toward defining and claiming my professional identity separate from her vision of who I would be.

She did not exert pressure that I become her image of me. She continued to offer opportunities, most of which I received enthusiastically, but she also recognized that I was separating and beginning to find my own way. Especially after the first 2 years of our relationship, I began to decline some of her invitations. She accepted this gracefully as part of the natural progression of my becoming independent and more confident in shaping my professional direction. She knew that mentoring ends and that the effectiveness of mentoring is related to the protégé's becoming self-assured, self-defined, and self-directed. She allowed the process of my letting go to unfold naturally as we began to shift roles and redefine our connection to one another.

A mentoring relationship involves coming together; experiencing a deep, emotional bond over time; and then recognizing the signs and the timing for separating and redefining the relationship, much like the process experienced in the counseling relationship. Transitional points of psychological and physical separation signal shifts in the mentoring relationship that are normative and developmental. The protégé moves from dependence to independence, from tentative and unsure to assertive and confident, from unaware and somewhat naive to savvy and sophisticated, and from being a protégé to readiness to be a mentor. Preparing to end the mentoring relationship is important for both mentor and protégé. The mentor has fulfilled the roles of preparing the protégé and can exit the relationship in order to move to mentoring a new protégé; the protégé moves to another level of personal and professional development and may become a mentor to others. The separation that occurs allows for a re-creation of the former relationship. A relationship will exist that differs contextually and in its degree of intensity and possibly proximity but, hopefully, will retain its deep interpersonal meaning and significance.

Unfortunately, mentoring relationships may not end in a functional, healthy, normative manner. Mentors and protégés may delay, resist, sabotage, extend, or prematurely terminate the natural ending of the relationship for professional and personal reasons. I attended a session at a professional counseling meeting in which the presenters had been mentor and protégé about 20 years earlier. Although both held equal professional status and were acknowledged professional leaders, the former mentor continued to exert his expert, teacher role, while his fellow presenter resumed his earlier learner role, acting as if he were still the graduate student. This imbalance was so apparent in the presentation that I said to the former protégé, a friend of mine, "You acted like his graduate student." He replied, "Yes, well, he treats me like his graduate student, and I guess it's easy for me to fall back into my role."

The mentor might have any number of issues with termination. They may include an unwillingness to relinquish the expert role, jealousy if the protégé's competence and reputation begin to exceed the mentor's, dependency on the protégé for successful completion of joint projects, overreliance on the protégé for emotional support and intimacy needs, overidentification with the protégé and the expectation that the protégé will follow the mentor's career path, or overextending the boundaries of the relationship to include wanting to assume a more personal role in the protégé's life. For example, a counseling mentor for a young child might have taken a surrogate parenting role and might resist terminating that connection. Likewise, the protégé might have issues about termination based on any number of reasons, such as fear of losing the support and approval of the mentor, dependency on the mentor for educational or career advancement, obligation to the mentor for the opportunities that the mentor has made available, fear of success and of outperforming the mentor, or guilt for not fulfilling the expectations that the mentor held for the protégé. A friend and I were discussing some of our regrets and feelings about our mentors. My friend noted that early in her career, an older woman, whom she revered greatly and was in awe of, had befriended her and became a mentor to her. The relationship lasted about a year and then gradually faded away over the next year. My friend said it took her some years to realize she had distanced herself and prematurely withdrawn from the relationship with her mentor for fear of not being "good enough" to deserve the time and attention of someone she so admired.

Ending mentoring relationships is perhaps the most complicated phase of the mentoring process. History has been written, a personal story exists between the mentor and the protégé, and lives have been changed by the course the mentoring relationship has taken. I recently witnessed a mentoring relationship that changed and was reshaped several times over 17 years. It is the most sacred ending to a mentoring relationship that I can imagine. It is a powerful story of mentoring and seems the most appropriate story for closing this chapter and this book.

A former mentor of many counseling professionals, myself included, Jean Cecil died in 1998 after 7 years of illness. Jean was a high school counselor and a director of guidance services in a rural county in West Virginia. She began her teaching career in counselor education at the University of Alabama in 1965 and was the chair of the Counselor Education Program from the early 1980s until she had a stroke that ended her career in 1991. She was the wise woman I named earlier whom I trusted would accept my decision not to go to a meeting she thought I should attend. Jean mentored many women and men over her career and received the Association for Counselor Education and Supervision's (ACES) Distinguished Mentoring Award in 1991, just 2 months before she had a stroke.

Jean conveyed warmth and support while leading with assertiveness and decisiveness. She was the model of professionalism and lived totally her commitment to counselor education. She was a scholar, teacher, and highly regarded professional leader. In the 1970s, she worked diligently within ACES to promote the creation of the Council for the Accreditation of Counseling and Related Educational Programs (CACREP). She avidly supported CACREP accreditation by serving as a consultant, site team trainer, site team chair, and researcher (e.g., Cecil & Comas, 1986). Jean became alarmed in the 1980s about the diminished visibility of school counseling preparation programs and brought national attention within ACES to revitalize school counseling preparation programs. In whatever she was doing professionally, Jean mentored others. Through involving, inviting, encouraging, and empowering others to grow professionally, Jean changed and strengthened the counseling profession.

After her stroke in 1991, she continued to be a mentor. This time she mentored us about life, about letting go, and about death. She taught us how to face the unexpected and to accept with grace and integrity the indignities that life can bring. Throughout her surgery, paralysis, rehabilitation, extended confinement, and eventual immobility, she modeled courage, strength, independence, resilience, and love. One of her former protégés said it seemed very fitting when Jean died on the Feast Day of the Guardian Angel.

Her funeral service was co-led by a former colleague, who had worked with her from 1965 until 1991, and a former doctoral student, who is a Catholic priest. Both had experienced Jean's mentoring. The priest shared his story of Dr. Jean's mentoring of him for 17 years. He recalled her encouragement, her challenges, and her correction of him as a master's student; her sitting by his side through the dissertation process; her walking beside him as they headed to his graduation; her willingly falling back to stand behind him as she hooded him "doctor"; and, finally, his walking across the stage on his own, knowing she was still there behind him, supporting and caring for him. I can think of no more poignant image of the fullness and depth of mentoring than his description of what Jean meant in his life.

Few of us may be graced enough to have such a mentoring connection in our lives, but we can hold that image of what mentoring means: to encourage, challenge, correct, sit and walk beside, and then to fall back willingly to allow the protégés to walk beyond. It is truly the picture of creating connected relationships that empower others.

References

Burlew, L. D. (1992). Multiple mentor model: A conceptual framework. *Journal of Career Development, 17,* 213–221.

Cecil, J. H., & Comas, R. E. (1986). Faculty perceptions of CACREP accreditation. *Counselor Education and Supervision, 25,* 237–245.

Egan, G. (1998). *The skilled helper* (6th ed.). Pacific Grove, CA: Brooks-Cole.

Epilogue

We hope you have enjoyed your journey through our book. Our purpose was to begin a discussion of the impact that successful mentoring relationships may have in the field of counseling. We hope you are excited about creating opportunities in which you are both mentor and protégé, using the mentoring relationships as ways to enrich your own lives and the lives of others. As counselors, we have the unique skills to capitalize on this powerful process, and we hope that this book stimulates further research and discussion related to mentoring, particularly in the counseling field.

You also may be left with unanswered questions. You may be thinking, "How do I find a mentor?" "Should I approach potential mentors or wait for mentoring relationships to develop in time?" The answers to these questions are unique to each mentor and protégé. Some mentoring relationships form naturally out of a mutual, unspoken commitment of mentor and protégé to each other. Other mentoring relationships are the result of the protégé actively seeking out a particular mentor and formally requesting guidance from that individual.

I believe the most important point to remember is not to wait for that life-changing mentor to find you. If there are individuals whom you think might be good mentors, be proactive and approach them. If the person does not seem receptive to establishing a formal relationship, then seek others who might. Also be aware of opportunities to cultivate existing relationships into mentoring relationships in a less formal way by using some of the strategies listed in the book, such as asking to collaborate on projects with the individual. Most important, remember the value of multiple mentors who may provide you with many different perspectives and experiences.

Finally, remember that mentors do not have to be perfect people. Seek opportunities to use your own unique gifts to connect with others. Everyone has the potential to benefit from a mentor, and everyone has the potential to be a mentor! As you read this book, we hope you thought of times when you needed a mentor and did not have one, and how that changed your life. We also hope you thought of times in your life when you needed a mentor and found one, and how that impacted who and where you are today. Hopefully, those thoughts will motivate you to look for opportunities to share yourself with others who may need a mentor. The experience will benefit both you and the protégé as you form connected, empowered relationships.

Index